ROBERT KETT AND
THE NORFOLK RISING

ROBERT KETT AND THE NORFOLK RISING

Joseph Clayton

Edited by Claire Dollman

ROBERT KETT
AND THE NORFOLK RISING

Joseph Clayton

First published in 1912
by Martin Secker

This edition first published in 2010
by
Mousehold Press
6, Constitution Opening
Norwich
NR3 4BD

Reprinted in 2019

Cover images from the mural by Piers Wallace
in the Castle Mall, Norwich,
reproduced by kind permission of the artist.

ISBN 987 1 874739 56 2

Printed by PageBros, Norwich

CONTENTS

Publisher's Note:

In 1549, Robert Kett, convicted of treason, was executed and his body left hanging in chains from the walls of Norwich castle. Precisely 400 years later a brass plaque was attached to those same walls announcing, '…this Memorial was placed here by the citizens of Norwich in reparation and honour to the memory of a notable leader in the long struggle of the common people of England to escape from a servile life into the freedom of just conditions.' And in 2008, Dr Ian Gibson, then MP for the Norwich North constituency that encompassed the scene of the rebellion, proposed an Early Day Motion calling on the Government to recognise that neither Robert Kett nor his brother William were traitors as charged. The motion failed to gather any signatures and went no further. If ever these two rebels were to be officially pardoned (they have certainly been pardoned in the court of public opinion) it would be the culmination of a process that began a century and a half ago which was to see the rehabilitation of their name.

For the best part of 300 years the official view of the rebellion had depicted it as unequivocal treason and its leader as the vilest of rebels who fully merited his fate. It was not until the nineteenth century that the events of 1549 began to be reinterpreted. Mid-century Chartists, and later, agricultural trade unionists and socialists came to see the uprising as prefiguring their own struggles against rural poverty, the power of landowners, and repressive legislation that prohibited collective organisation, and its leader as a man to be admired.

Joseph Clayton (b.1868) worked within that radical tradition. An independent historian, elected to a fellowship of the Royal Historical Society in 1920, his list of publications indicate his interests: trade union, co-operatives and labour history, and Christian socialism. Robert Kett and the Norfolk Rising (published in 1912) was dedicated to John Burns, one of the three working class men elected as Independents to the Commons in 1892, and it indicates that together they had undertaken a 'joint pilgrimage to the scenes of the Norfolk rising'. His book was the first account that sought to justify the rebellion and to offer an heroic portrait of Kett. Its introduction concluded: 'The enterprise of Robert Kett and the doings at his camp at Norwich, and the deeds of the brave fellows of his company, have never had full justice done to them.'

In reissuing *Robert Kett and the Norfolk Rebellion* we have lightly edited the original text. Clayton made frequent use of the early accounts, splicing verbatim sixteenth-century English into his own natural Edwardian phrasing. The mixture did not always make for comfortable reading. We have paraphrased some of these sections to make for a more consistent style and one that is easier for the contemporary reader.

Acknowledgements: we wish to express our thanks to Nicole Fassihi for researching the illustrations used in this edition; Norma Watt, archivist at the Norwich Castle Museum and Art Gallery; Piers Wallace for allowing us to reproduce sections of his mural designed for the Castle Mall; and Karen Fuller for her technical expertise with the scans for the cover.

PREFACE
to the 1912 edition

The story of the uprising of the country people of Norfolk, under the leadership of Robert Kett, in 1549, is of more than local interest. The story is immortal for lovers of English liberty. It was an agrarian war, this uprising, waged by the peasants, with courage and with characteristic good temper and moderation, against their enemies the landowners. The ferocity displayed in the peasant insurrections in France and Germany is conspicuously absent in the 'Kett Rebellion'. As in 1381 under Wat Tyler, and 1450 under Jack Cade, an English peasantry driven to revolt could put up a good fight against intolerable conditions without any implacable hatred for their antagonists. The annals of these three great popular risings are not stained with the blood of murdered landowners. It is the peasants themselves who are sacrificed when their effort has failed., The enmity of the poor for the rich is a very rare and feeble thing compared with the dislike and contempt of the rich for the poor. (If it had ever been otherwise revolt might have become revolution.) The poor and the great mass of landless working folk in England have never made common cause against the wealthy and the landlords, while the latter, with a few heroic exceptions, have always stood together in close phalanx against the demands of the peasants. To-day it is with savage animosity and bitter impatience that the wealthy speak from the fulness of their hearts of the working people when the latter give trouble by going on strike. At other times, when the strike is forgotten, the tone is kindly contempt for obvious inferiors.

There is neither such hatred nor scorn in the heart of the average peasant or town worker; and there never has been in England.

Kett's rebellion was suppressed by foreign mercenaries, but it lasted six weeks, and had its crowded hours of glorious life.

The enterprise of Robert Rett and the doings at his camp at Norwich, and the deeds of the brave fellows of his company, have never had full justice done to them.

As far as possible I have told the story in the words of the earliest narratives, only in every case the spelling has been changed to modern use.

J. C.
Hampstead, 1911

I

THE CAUSE OF THE RISING

In truth, the enclosures themselves, whereby vast numbers of poor people (whose right it was) had the food taken out of their mouths by the rich, were the causes of tumults. – Sir John Hayward, *Life of Edward VI*. Note by John Strype

During the period, which may be roughly defined as from 1450 to 1550, enclosure meant to a large extent the actual dispossession of the tenants by their manorial lords. This took place either in the form of the violent ousting of the sitting tenant, or of a refusal on the death of one tenant to admit the son, who in earlier centuries would have been treated as his natural successor. Proofs abound.
– W. J. Ashley, *Economic History*

Marry, for these enclosures do undo us all, for they make us pay dearer for our land that we occupy, and cause that we can have no land in manner for our money to put to tillage; all is taken up for pastures, either for sheep or for grazing of cattle. So that I have known of late a dozen ploughs within less compass than six miles about me laid down within these seven years, and where forty persons had their livings, now one man and his shepherd hath all. Which thing is not the least cause of these uproars, for by these enclosures men do lack living and be idle, and therefore for very necessity they are desirous of a change, being in hope to come thereby to somewhat, and well assured, howsoever it befall with them, it cannot be harder with them than it was before. – *Discourse of this Commonweal of this Realm of England, 1581*

CHAPTER I:

The Cause of the Rising

The land enclosures made by the landlords provoked the Norfolk Rising of 1549. The country people, dispossessed of their holdings, were driven to revolt. They would 'take arms, and mix heaven and earth together, rather than endure such great cruelty', according to the 'Complaint' of Kett and his rebels.

These enclosures, first noticeable towards the end of the fifteenth century, took two forms, both equally destructive to the existence of an agricultural population. Firstly, 'Engrossing' – the concentration of many holdings by one person and the decay of the other holdings. By this process half-a-dozen farms would be absorbed by one landowner and worked by him, or by a tenant of his from one residence, the other five dwelling-houses being pulled down. Secondly, the actual enclosure of lands previously held in common by the peasants and the appropriation of these lands for the exclusive use of the landowner. In both cases the result was the same – arable land was turned into pasture and the people were evicted.

It was not so much the enclosing of common land, as the vast untilled commons were not invaded seriously by the landowners until the middle of the eighteenth century. It was this engrossing of homesteads, concentrating many holdings under one hand, the seizure of fields from the peasants and taking these fields out of cultivation, that broke up the old country life of England. Before this, England had been mainly a nation of small farmers. The land was open country; the hedgerows, so long a joy to us in spring and summer, were unknown.

With the discovery made towards the end of the fifteenth century, that sheep and cattle were more profitable to the landowner than small tenants, came a new view of land tenure. This was because the demand for wool in the markets was constant and steady and less labour was required when grazing took the place of tillage.

A new concept of land ownership was rising, subject to the same complete control and use as any personal property. This was in contrast to the feudal or communal notion of the Middle Ages.[1] Under the old view land was regarded not as a source of wealth but as a source of men. It was more important for the lord to have men to defend him than for him to increase his wealth by extracting as much rent as he could from his tenants.[2] The new view naturally prevailed. There was no power strong enough to withstand the landlords (always the real rulers of an agricultural nation) when they got rid of the people from the land and proceeded to bring in more and more sheep.

Laws were passed and royal proclamations were issued to prohibit enclosures, but these were in vain as the proclamations were unheeded. Acts of Parliament were passed in 1489 and 1515 against the 'pulling down of towns' and the restoration of tillage in pasture lands. Whole villages were being destroyed and their populations evicted by the enclosures. Royal Commissions enquired into the enclosures and issued reports in 1517 and 1549, and Royal proclamations denounced these enclosures in 1518, 1526, 1548 and 1549. Sixteenth century writers and preachers, of all schools, declaimed eloquently and bitterly against the misery of a people cut off from access to the land.

Sir Thomas More in the first part of his *Utopia,* 1516, puts the case as he saw it:

> For look in what parts of the realm doth grow the finest and therefore dearest wool, there noblemen and gentlemen, yea, and certain abbots, holy men, no doubt, not contenting themselves with the yearly revenues and profits that were wont to grow to their forefathers and predecessors of their lands, nor being content that they live in rest and pleasure – nothing profiting, yea, much annoying the

public weal leave no ground for tillage, they enclose all into pastures; they throw down houses; they pluck down towns and leave nothing standing but only the church to be made a sheepfold...They turn all dwelling-places and all glebe land into desolation and wilderness. Therefore, that one covetous and insatiable cormorant may compass about and inclose many thousand acres of ground together within one pale or hedge, the husbandmen be thrust out of their own, or else either by cunning or fraud, or by violent oppression, or by wrongs and injuries they be so wearied, that they be compelled to sell all. By one means therefore or another, either by hook or by crook, they must needs depart away, men, women, husbands, wives, fatherless children, widows, mothers, with their young babies, and their whole household, small in substance and large in number, as husbandry requireth many hands. Away they trudge, I say, out of their known and accustomed houses, finding no place to rest in...And when they have wandered abroad till the little they have be spent, what can they then else do but steal, and then justly be hanged, or else go about a begging.

In his *Complaint of Roderick Moss* (1542) Brinklow, a fierce Protestant, writes about 'the inordinate enhancing of rents and taking of unreasonable fines.' He speaks about the misery wrought by the new landlords who had succeeded to the abbey lands, and who, 'for every trifle, even for his friends' pleasure, if the tenant have not a lease shall put him out of his farm.'

Preaching before Edward VI Thomas Lever, Master of St John's, Cambridge, exclaims:

It is the common custom with covetous landlords to let their housing so decay that the farmer shall be fain for a small reward or none at all, to give up his lease: that they (the landlords), taking the ground into their own hands, may turn all into pasture. So now old fathers, poor widows, and young children lie begging in the streets.

Latimer, in 1548, is no less emphatic in his judgment on the landowners:

You landlords, you rent-raisers, I may say you step lords, you have for your possession too much. That which heretofore went for £20 or £40 by the year, which is an honest portion to be had gratis in one lordship of another man's sweat and labour, now is let for £50 or £100 by the year; and thus is caused such dearth that poor men which live of their labour cannot with the sweat of their faces have a living. I tell you, my lords and masters, this is not for the King's honour .... If the King's honour, as some men say, standeth in the multitude of people, then these graziers, enclosers, rent-raisers, are hinderers of the King's honour; for whereas have been a great many householders and inhabitants, there is now but a shepherd and his dog. My lords and masters, such proceedings do intend plainly to make of the yeomanry slavery.

Latimer's reference to his father's holding has often been quoted, but will bear repetition:

My father was a yeoman, and had no lands of his own, only he had a farm of £3 or £4 a year at the uttermost, and hereupon he tilled so much as kept half-a-dozen men. He had walk for 100 sheep, and my mother milked 30 kine ... He that now hath it, payeth £16 by year or more, and is not able to do anything for his Prince, for himself, nor for his children, or give a cup of drink to the poor.

Bishop Scory, writing to Edward VI, estimates the land thrown out of cultivation at two acres out of three:

To trust to have as much upon one acre as was wont to grow upon three – for I think that the tillage is not now above that rate, if it be so much – is but a vain expectation. A great number of the people are so pined and famished by reason of the great scarcity and dearth that the great sheep masters have brought into this noble realm, that they are become more like the slavery and peasantry of France than the ancient and godly yeomanry of England.[3]

Still the enclosures went on unchecked, and yeomanry and peasantry dwindled and disappeared from the face of the land in many parishes. The confiscation of the monasteries, followed by the ruination of every kind of charitable foundation and the seizure of the properties of the guilds, greatly increased the miseries.

To the successors of the monks and friars land was purely capital, making them harsher landlords and sharper business men in every way. The contemporary evidence is again overwhelming. Brinklow called the monks 'imps of Antichrist', but confessed that 'they never enhanced their lands, nor took so cruel fines as do our temporal tyrants.' Lever, Latimer, and Bernard Gilpin all give similar testimony.

By the middle of the sixteenth century the old landmarks were gone. The monasteries were ended and their hospitality went with them. The parish churches were stripped of the ornaments the people had provided and the funds of the guilds had been seized. To realise what that meant we have only to imagine the Government of our day forbidding all friendly societies, trade unions and co-operative societies and annexing their properties. The Church of England had been separated from the rest of Catholic Christendom and the new Prayer Books of Edward VI substituted for the old familiar services of Mass and Evensong. As Pollard comments:

The foundations upon which society had been based for 500 years were broken up, the ideas which dominated it passed away, and those which were to regulate the new society were still without form and void. The change was neither begun nor ended during the Tudor period, but that age felt more severely than any other the stress and the shock of the revolution.[4]

The increase in national wealth was achieved by the pauperisation of large sections of the community, a condition that was reproduced at the beginning of the nineteenth century. This is inevitable when, at every fresh improvement in labour-saving machinery, the people are landless. A debased coinage, the rise in prices and the fall in wages all added to the agony of the working people at the beginning of Edward VI's reign. Froude summed up the distress of the country people:

> It remains certain that the absorption of the small farms, the enclosure system, and the increase of grazing farms had assumed proportions mischievous and dangerous. Leases as they fell in could not obtain renewal: the copyholder, whose farm had been held by his forefathers so long that custom seemed to have made it his own, found his fines or his rent quadrupled, or himself without alternative expelled. The Act against the pulling down of farmhouses had been evaded by the repair of a room which might be occupied by a shepherd; a single furrow would be driven across a meadow of a hundred acres, to prove that it was still under the plough. The great cattle-owners, to escape the sheep statutes, held their stock in the names of their sons or servants; the highways and the villages were covered, in consequence, with forlorn and outcast families, now reduced to beggary, who had been the occupiers of comfortable holdings; and thousands of dispossessed tenants made their way to London, clamouring in the midst of their starving children at the doors of the courts of law for redress which they could not obtain.[5]

The harshness and greed of landlords was no longer restrained by religion or any sense of social obligation; they were bent only on getting rich as quickly as possible. They had their counterpart in the unscrupulous energies of the traders. Fraud was rife in the towns and Parliament was as impotent to deal with these prosperous business men as it was to stop the enclosures.

Paget, writing to Protector Somerset, found neither religion nor law in the land:

> Society in a realm doth consist and is maintained by means of religion and law, and these two or one wanting, farewell all just society, government, justice. I fear at home is neither. The use of the old religion is forbidden, the use of the new is not yet printed in the stomachs of eleven or twelve parts of the realm.[6]

Yet, if law was despised by landowners, it could still be made effective against the poor. In Henry VIII's reign Parliament brought in the lash and the gallows to solve the unemployed problem. Punishment seemed the right thing for homeless and landless people, peasants dispossessed of holdings, or soldiers broken in the French Wars.

In 1531 an Act of Parliament ordered a whipping for all unlicensed beggers. Five years later, in the year of the suppression of the lesser monasteries, Parliament, finding the unemployed still alive, decided to deal more radically with the problem. On the first conviction of unemployment all vagrants, men and women alike, were to be whipped; for the second offence they were to be mutilated; and on the third conviction they were to be hanged as felons.

The Act of 1536 was rigidly enforced and thousands of unemployed men and women suffered the full penalty of the law. And still the unemployed problem remained unsolved, so it was believed only by sterner measures and greater severity could the question be settled. In 1547, the first year of Edward VI, an Act was passed selling the unemployed into slavery. For a first conviction branding and two years of slavery was ordered for the unemployed vagrant; the slave was to be beaten and chained by his master and for running away he was to be further branded and adjudged a slave forever. Death as a felon was the penalty for a third conviction.

Even this drastic measure failed to rid the country of the unemployed. It seemed government had got rid of papal authority only to bring back slavery to England. So in 1549 the Act of 1547 was repealed and the Act of 1531 was once more the law of the land.

In 1549 came the great risings in the West of England and in Norfolk, and many smaller risings elsewhere. Robert Kett, the Norfolk leader, believed that Protector Somerset would order something more hopeful for the peasants than hanging and flogging. The landowners, however, were totally distrustful of the Protector's plans. As it turned out, Somerset accomplished nothing for the peasants and only ruin for himself. His policy merely encouraged the yeomen and peasants to hope for redress of their wrongs, just as it angered the landowners.

In the heyday of his power Cardinal Wolsey had also attempted to save the countryside from the growing power of the landlords. His inquiry of 1517 included the counties of Oxford, Buckinghamshire, Northampton, Berkshire, and Warwickshire, and reported large enclosures of common lands and the eviction of several hundred people. Restitution was ordered to be made for all enclosures carried out since 1485 and the King's pardon could be requested. That was where the matter ended as the landowners neither restored lands, nor stopped enclosing them. At the dissolution of monasteries so many estates were enlarged that for a few years common lands were left untouched in many places. However, on the death of Henry VIII there was a vigorous renewal of enclosures.

Where Wolsey had failed it was unlikely that Somerset could succeed, especially at a time of social anarchy, with the nation distracted by a violent revolution in religion. Besides, Somerset was hardly the man to accomplish the work he proposed as his own annexations of Church lands were notorious. A parish church and part of St Paul's Cathedral were sacrificed for the building of Somerset House. This, and his support of the poor, infuriated his enemies on the Council, notably the Earl of Warwick.

On 1st June 1548 the Proclamation against enclosures was issued, and within a few weeks Commissioners were sent down into the counties of Oxford, Berks, Warwick, Bedford, Leicester, Buckingham and Northampton. These commissioners included Fulke Greville, Sir Francis Russell and John Hales. They were sent to make inquiries into the number of acres enclosed or converted from arable to pasture since 1485, and to disclose the names of all who kept more than 2,000 sheep, or who had broken the law.[7]

'Let the Commissioners do their duty bravely, and the world would be honest again,' Somerset wrote with brave optimism:

> The great fines for lands would abate, all things would wax cheap; twenty and thirty eggs would again be sold for a penny, as in times past; the poor craftsmen could live and sell their wares at reasonable prices; and the noblemen and gentlemen who had not enhanced their rents would be able once more to maintain hospitality.

The Commission, welcomed by the yeomen and peasants, was frustrated by the landowners. John Hales, the one man really zealous for the people, wrote bitterly to Somerset concerning the attitude of the landowners and the methods used to prevent the facts being published:

> After the King's Majesty had sent forth the proclamation and commission, what did they not to hinder it? Some found the means to have their servants sworn in the Juries, to the intent to have them hazard their souls to save their greediness. And as I have learned since, it is not possible in any of the Shires where we were, to make a jury without

them, such is the multitude of Retainers and hangers-on. Which thing if it be not remedied the King shall be sure never to have his laws truly executed ... Some poor men were threatened to be put from their holds if they presented, some also as I farther learned have no certainty of their holds which were wont to be let by copy for life and otherwise for years, because they at no time nor in nothing should offend their landlords but do and say whatsoever they will command them. As it pleaseth my landlord, so shall it be! A godly hearing in the commonwealth! Some also were indicted because they presented the truth, and some were persuaded that the end of the commission should be but a money matter, as it had been in times past. I could declare unto you a great many slights wherewith some of them thought to have blinded us and the presenters, but for very shame I will let them pass.[8]

Hales also brought in three Agrarian Bills in Parliament, for the rebuilding of houses fallen into decay and for the maintenance of tillage and husbandry. The first bill was introduced in the House of Lords and quickly rejected. The second passed the Lords, but was lost in the Commons. The third, introduced in the Commons, never reached the Lords.

The report of the Commissioners, a petition to Parliament, declared the population diminished, the farmer and labourer impoverished, villages destroyed, towns decayed and the labouring classes reduced to great suffering. It urged that landowners should not farm any portion of their estates beyond the needs of their households; that the great farms should be broken up; and that a moderate fine of ten marks be exacted from those breaking the law concerning enclosures.

But Parliament did nothing and the landlords ignored the Commission and its report. The only result of Somerset's policy was a growing restlessness amongst the country people and his own unpopularity with the nobility.

In the spring of 1549 Somerset ordered another commission to enforce the Enclosure Acts and issued another proclamation. He claimed that the people were now 'plucking down pales, hedges and ditches at their pleasure'. To stop this disorder Somerset promised that the commission should redress their wrongs. He also announced a pardon to the 'rude and ignorant people who, in certain shires of England, had done great and most perilous and heinous disorder, and had riotously assembled themselves, plucked down men's hedges, disparked their parks, and taken upon them the King's power and sword, but had now repented of their evil doings.' At the same time death was threatened to anyone who made similar disturbances after this.[9]

Sir William Paget told Somerset plainly that this lenient policy was wrong:

> Your pardons have given evil men a boldness to enterprise, and cause them to think you dare not meddle with them, but are glad to please them, and to suffer whatsoever they list, and what pleaseth them, be it right or wrong, they must have it.

Writing again early in July Paget still harps on the same point:

> I told your Grace the truth, and was not believed: well, now your Grace seeth it, what saith your Grace? Marry, the King's subjects are out of all discipline, out of obedience, caring neither for Protector nor King, and much less for any other mean officer. And what is the cause? Your own levity, your softness, your opinion to be good to the poor. The opinion of such as saith to your Grace, 'Oh, Sir, there was never man that had the hearts of the poor as you have. Oh! the commons pray for you, sir: they say, God save your life.' I know your gentle heart right well, and that your meaning is good and godly: howsoever, some evil men list to prate here that you have some greater enterprise in your head, that lean so much to the multitude. I know,

I say, your good meaning and honest nature. But I say, sir, is it great pity (as the common proverb goeth in a warm summer) that ever fair weather should do harm. It is pity that your so much gentleness should be an occasion of so great an evil as is now chanced in England by these rebels .... Where is the law used in England at liberty? Almost nowhere. The foot taketh upon him the part of the head, and commons is become a king, appointing conditions and laws to the governors, saying, 'Grant this and that, and we will go home.' 10

Paget had been in alliance with Somerset from the death of Henry VIII, and he warned him of the natural hatred of the lords of the Council to any sympathy the Government had with the peasants. His proposed cure for the disorders was that the Council should meet and the German mercenaries be recalled from Calais. Lord Ferris and Sir William Herbert should also be sent for from Wales with as many men as they could bring, and the Protector, along with the chief justices of England, should go with as many noblemen and others as possible into the disaffected counties. There he should capture twenty or thirty of the worst offenders of the shire and the six 'rankest knaves' be hanged and the rest remain in prison.

But when this letter was written Cornwall and Devon were in open revolt against the new Prayer Book and the new form of Church service which the people likened to a Christmas game. Meanwhile in Norfolk, the great uprising under Robert Kett had already commenced.

Somerset had openly showed support for the people since the covetousness of the gentlemen had given them occasion to rise. He believed it was better for them to die than perish for lack of living. But the nobles and country gentlemen, furious at the attempts of Somerset to restore the enclosed land and at the boldness of the peasants, repulsed the latter by force of arms.

It seems plain that Robert Kett, together with many of the country folk, were convinced that Somerset was with them against the landlords. But by July 1549 Somerset was tottering to his fall. He could neither support the rebels nor recover their allegiance. As he was strongly Protestant, the Catholic Rising in Cornwall and Devon was particularly abhorrent to him. Riots to enforce the laws against enclosures were one thing, but an open rebellion, whether religious or purely agrarian, was another. The Protector won the hatred of the Earl of Warwick and the landowners by his commissions and proclamations against enclosures. He also lost all favour with the mass of people by the inevitable savagery which followed the suppression of the risings.

In the first half of the sixteenth century the people rose in revolt over and over again. Sometimes against the Government changes in the Church services, more often against the social and economic changes that were depopulating rural England. The 'Pilgrimage of Grace' in 1536, and the rising in the West in 1549, were the chief demonstrations against the destruction of the old order in religion. However, they were no more successful than the social revolts.

In 1527 and 1529 bad harvests followed by famine provoked agrarian riots in Norfolk. In 1537 at Walsingham, Sir Nicholas Myleham, George Gysborough and others attempted an insurrection, hoping to remedy the poverty that prevailed. The rising was put down before anything was done and at Aylsham, one Elizabeth Wood was arrested in connection with this revolt. This was for saying:

It was pity that these Walsingham men were discovered,
for we shall never have a good world till we fall together
by the ears:
'And with clubs and clouted shoon
Shall the deed be done'
for we had never had a good world since this King reigned.

Myleham and Gysborough were executed at Norwich but the

fate of Elizabeth Wood is not recorded.

In 1540, John Walker of Griston set about rousing the people to the following effect:

> If three or four good fellows would ride in the night with every man a bell, and cry in every town that they pass through, "To Swaffham! To Swaffham!" by the morning there would be 10,000 assembled at the least; and then one bold fellow to stand forth and say, 'Sirs, now we be here assembled: you know how all the gentlemen in manner be gone forth, and you know how little favour they bear to us poor men: let us therefore now go home to their houses, and there shall we have harness, substance, and victual. And as many as will not turn to us, let us kill them, yea, even their children in the cradles: for it were a good thing if there were no more gentlemen in Norfolk than there be white bulls.

However, these somewhat forcible proposals were not carried out, and John Walker paid the penalty for his free opinions.

These years with their petty outbreaks all gave evidence of the general unrest, and in the long pent-up sense of injury culminated in the Kett Rebellion of 1549. The Rebellion itself failed in the end, but it is distinguished from other agrarian revolts by the serious efforts made by its leaders to establish some sort of social commonwealth. Kett made no march on London, as Wat Tyler and Jack Cade had done, but he did set up a real tribunal, rough but effective, of law and order in the camp at Norwich. There was confidence, misplaced but sincere, that Protector Somerset would treat the rising with consideration.

In July 1549, Cornwall and Devon were ablaze for the return of the Mass in the parish churches, with priests hanging from countless church towers and steeples, not only in the West but also in Oxfordshire. Meanwhile, the peasants were taking the law into their own hands in Somerset, Lincoln, Essex, Kent, Wiltshire and Buckinghamshire. Because of this unrest it was impossible for the Protector to countenance an armed insurrection in Norfolk however fiercely the fires of the insurrection had been fanned by years of misgovernment. Had the people ever been so driven to take up arms for life and liberty as were the English country folk in that year of 1549?

II

THE BEGINNING OF THE RISING

'The occasion of this rebellion was because divers lords and gentlemen, who were possessed of abbey lands and other large commons and waste grounds, had caused many of those commons and wastes to be enclosed, whereby the poor and indigent people were much offended, because thereby abridged of the liberty that they formerly had to common cattle, etc., on the said grounds to their own advantage.' – Blomefield, *History of Norfolk*

'By bearing a confident countenance in all his actions, the Vulgars took him (Kett) to be both valiant and wise, and a fit man to be their commander.' – Sir John Hayward, *Life of Edward VI*

CHAPTER II:

The Beginning of the Rising

The rising began at Attleborough on 20th June 1549. Here one John Green, lord of the Manor of Wilby, had set up fences and hedges around the common lands of Harpham and Attleborough that belonged to his manor. Hearing that the men of Kent had filled up ditches and pulled down fences, the inhabitants of Attleborough, Eccles and Wilby and other neighbouring villages assembled together and vowed they would do the same in Norfolk. Straight away they knocked down Squire Green's hedges and reopened the whole area that had previously been common land.

The people were without leaders and without organisation. However, they were in dire straits, and could see nothing for it but to take the matter into their own hands. So the fire was kindled.

A fortnight and more passed, and on 7th July came the annual feast at Wymondham. People gathered from far and near and a play was performed in honour of the festival of St Thomas of Canterbury, to whom a chapel in the middle of the town was dedicated. Henry VIII had removed the name of St Thomas from the calendar and the funds of all the guilds had been confiscated, but the old Church plays would still be performed in some towns and villages for years to come. The people collected in great numbers in the town on the Saturday night, before the feast on Sunday. There was talk of the enclosures, of the ruin and beggary overtaking the land, and of the unrest at Attleborough. The spirit of revolt spread quickly. If the old common rights were to be saved then the people must act promptly, as every day saw fresh invasions and the planting of new hedges to keep the peasants off the land.

On the Monday, the play ended and the fair over, a great body of people set off to destroy the fences set up at Morley by Master Hobart. They then proceeded to Hethersett, a few miles down the

Norwich road, where Sergeant Flowerdew had enclosed many areas of common land.

Flowerdew was an old enemy who had fallen into disrepute with his neighbours ten years before the rising. When Henry VIII had ordered the destruction of the abbey at Wymondham the people there, wishing to save their noble church, petitioned the King that they would pay for the bells, lead and so on according to their value. Henry consented and the people paid the money, believing thereby to have saved their church. But, it would seem this good intent was frustrated by Sergeant Flowerdew, who stripped the church of its lead and took all the freestone from the south cross aisle, which he then completely demolished[1]. Naturally, by this action Flowerdew had won the hatred of all who had worked and paid for the preservation of the church, including the Ketts who had been conspicuous subscribers. This confirmed the Ketts as Flowerdew's enemy.

No sooner had the people begun to pull down Flowerdew's fences at Hethersett than the cunning lawyer suggested to the leaders of the invasion that they should attack the Ketts who had also made enclosures, at Wymondham. Flowerdew even paid the rioters 40 pence on condition that they destroy Robert Kett's enclosure. It was therefore at Flowerdew's prompting that Robert Kett was drawn into the rising.

Robert Kett and his brother William were craftsmen. Robert is described as a tanner, and William as a butcher and a mercer. They were from an ancient family and both men of substance. Robert Kett rented three manors from the Earl of Warwick, near Wymondham; William had purchased two properties, Westwode Chapel and Chossell's Manor. Robert's estate was valued at 1,000 marks, and his yearly income at £50. For three centuries the Ketts had lived in Norfolk and since 1483 had been one of the most important families in Wymondham. But wealthy landowners as they were, when the call came, Robert and William Kett did not shrink from joining with the peasantry in the war against enclosures. They did more than this, they boldly put themselves at the head of the revolt and gave their lives for the cause they espoused.

Robert Kett must have pondered the evil plight of the commonwealth of England, as other men were doing in the anarchy of Edward VI's reign. It must have seemed to him that Protector Somerset was in earnest about checking the enclosures that were desolating the countryside, and that the people were right to enforce their demands for the old rights of commoning. The news had reached him of the events at Attleborough and of the unrest all around. At present the tumult was a local affair, not differing greatly from the many other disturbances at that time in Norfolk. Was this rising to be put down by the strong arm of authority? Or was it possible that all East Anglia would rise, and that the young King and his minister would listen to the complaints of the people and redress their wrongs? Could the rising achieve its purpose and end the oppression of the peasantry?

One thing was plain to Robert Kett – the people lacked leadership and good counsel, and without this no rising could be successful. The movement was spreading. Wisely led, the courage and resolution of the country people could accomplish much, but organisation and discipline were imperative. It was perhaps a forlorn hope to take up arms in the cause of a landless peasantry, but they believed in Protector Somerset's sympathy with the cause. To lead the rising meant, for Kett, giving up the quiet yeoman's life at Wymondham and plunging into the strenuous responsibilities of an insurgent camp, exchanging pleasant domestic ease for the thousand-and-one dangers and difficulties of open rebellion.

No great promise of riches or glory or honour was offered to the Ketts should the rising be successful. They would make no personal gain, and no private wrongs of their own called for redress. Victory could but bring the satisfaction of a fight bravely fought, of the goodwill of poorer neighbours well earned, and of a decisive blow struck at the evils of the time. Kett had a vision of a fairer and happier England, where the pride of the rich should no longer oppress the poor, and all should live in neighbourly and brotherly friendship.

It was the old gospel of social revolution, preached by John Ball and the leaders of the Peasants' Revolt in the fourteenth century, that inspired Robert Kett and drew him irresistibly when the time came. In 1381 Geoffrey Litster and many other Norfolk men had gone to their deaths seeking the establishment of a social commune. Should the rising fail it would be, at worst, no more for Kett than the sacrifice of his life in a good cause.

If they had sought to save their lives by avoiding and discouraging their landless neighbours in revolt, the Ketts would have remained unknown, indistinguishable from other landowners and dead for all time as far as history is concerned. By losing their lives willingly for the people they have gained an immortality, as the story of the 'Kett Rebellion' fills a famous page in English history. The heroism of its leaders will be acclaimed as long as the love of brave deeds shall endure in England.

The Ketts did not instigate the rising. They seemed no different from other landowners, even making enclosures, until the people called upon them for help. But they were men of strong convictions, passionately hating injustice and ready for action. Ambition which clutches at sovereignty and rule may be despicable, but even more despicable is the weakness of leadership at times of peril or those that shrink from taking command for fear of trouble.

With a full sense of responsibility, Robert Kett answered the crowd that gathered at his house at Wymondham on the evening of 8th July. He would pull down his own enclosures at once, but more than that, he would join with them whole-heartedly in the removal of all enclosures and together they would break the power of their enemies. From the beginning the rising was, in Kett's eyes, a social crusade against the dominion of landlords, and this speech at the very beginning of his captaincy strikes the confident note of revolutionary enthusiasm:

> I am ready, and will be ready at all times, to do whatsoever, not only to repress, but to subdue the power of great men; and I hope to bring it to pass ere long that as ye shall repent of your painful labour, so shall these, the great ones, of their pride.

Many horrible things of late years have ye endured, with many wrongs and miseries have ye been vexed and afflicted.

But I will that ye be of good cheer, for this so great severity, so exceeding covetousness, and so seldom heard of cruelty in all sorts, seem to be hated and accursed of God and men. Moreover, I promise that the hurts done unto the public weal and the common pasture by the importunate lords thereof shall be revenged.

Whatsoever lands I have enclosed shall again be made common unto ye and all men, and my own hands shall first perform it.

Then, to bring the speech to an end, Kett announces his willingness to lead the revolt:

Never shall I be wanting where your good is concerned. You shall have me, if you will, not only as a companion, but as a captain; and in the doing of the so great a work before us, not only as a fellow, but for a leader, author, and principal. Not only will I be present at all your consultations, but, if you will have it so, always will I be your president.[2]

There were great shouts of rejoicing at these words and the enthusiasm became contagious. People surrounded Kett and hailed him excitedly as their leader. Fired with his spirit they believed a new day was dawning, for here was a landowner willingly helping to lay open the enclosures he had made and promising to do more. When such things happened it must have seemed that the time was ripe for change in England.

The work of destroying the fences and filling up ditches was renewed with vigour. Before nightfall Flowerdew, at Hetherset, was maddened by the knowledge that his 40 pence had been spent in vain, to the very opposite of his intentions, as the people left Wymondham to level his enclosures. The irate Sergeant could only curse Kett as a pest to his country, abuse him as the leader of a group of vagabonds and endeavour to discredit him with his new followers. The idea was started that Kett was withdrawing from the revolt, but to those not at Wymondham it was a mere rumour that Robert Kett was joining with the rioters at all.

All were reassured the next day (9th July) when Kett answered those who came to beg him to remain their friend. He promised to assist them utterly and be faithful to the office bestowed upon him.

> I will never lay down the charge which the commonwealth has committed to me, until your rights have been won, nor is anything more dear to me than your welfare. Before all things else do I put your welfare and deliverance, and for these I am willing to spend not only my goods, but my very life, so dear to me is the cause in which we are embarked.[3]

Then it was announced that William Kett, whose courage and daring were widely known, had decided to stand with his brother Robert. Rumour gave way to a definite declaration that the Ketts were in command, and that a movement was already being made and organised.

From the moment they gave themselves to the rising, the Ketts lost no time. In hot haste the march began. They took the highroad to Norwich, crossing the river at Cringleford, and spent the night at Bowthorpe. Every hour saw fresh additions to the army; crowds of desperate men, servants and numbers of unemployed flocked to join their fellows.

Up to this point the authorities had taken no heed of what was happening, but Sir Edmund Windham, High Sheriff of Norfolk, came to Bowthorpe. He proclaimed the people there to be rebels, commanding them to depart peaceably to their own homes. Nevylle reports that, had his horsemanship not been better than his rhetoric, he would never have left the place alive as the people were greatly offended by his speech. They attempted to seize him but he managed to flee on horseback and escape to Norwich.[4]

The temper of the people was rising. That same night many came in from the surrounding country and from the city, bringing all the weapons they could lay their hands on. Kett delivered a fierce harangue against the tyranny of the landowners:

> Now are ye overtopped and trodden down by gentlemen, and put out of possibility ever to recover foot. Rivers of riches ran into the coffers of your landlords, while you are pared to the quick and fed upon pease and oats like beasts. You are fleeced by these landlords for their private benefit, and as well kept under by the public burdens of State wherein, while the richer sort favour themselves, ye are gnawn to the very bones. Your tyrannous masters often implead, arrest, and cast you into prison, so that they may the more terrify and torture you in your minds and wind your necks more surely under their arms. And then they palliate these pillories with the fair pretence of law and authority! Fine workmen, I warrant you, are this law and authority, who can do their dealings so closely that men can only discover them for your undoing. Harmless counsels are fit for tame fools; for you who have already stirred there is no hope but in adventuring boldly.

It was plain to Robert Kett that the only cure for the social distress was to abolish once and for all the ascendancy of the landlord class, and to make England a free commonwealth. Either the people must defeat the landlords or very soon the landlords would have the whole land in their possession, and the people would be held in hopeless subjection. Acts of Parliament had already been passed making actual 'slaves' of the poor, landless folk who walked the roads; men and women driven to vagabondage by the enclosures of the common lands and the destruction of tillage in the old common fields. And Parliament was, only this year, making it high treason for twelve or more persons to meet together, and calling it felony to break down the enclosures that were at the root of all the misery.

Yet, for all his hatred of mastery and thraldom and his love of social equality and brotherhood, Kett was, by nature, a law-abiding man. All through the rising his authority was exerted to maintain obedience to orders, to keep discipline in the ranks and to curb all anarchy.

'The Rebels' Complaint', which was issued at this time, was the manifesto of the labouring agricultural people of Kett's army. Whether drawn up by Robert Kett himself or by some unknown scribe, it is full of the spirit of social revolt that animated all Kett's utterances. At the beginning of the rising only about a thousand men set out with Kett. But they were men of resolution, men of clear conviction that the wrongs and miseries of their age were intolerable, and that it was better to strive and die, if need be, for liberty rather than pass the days in dull despair and shameful servitude. The older men had seen the state of things get steadily worse for the country folk. The peasants were suffering under the pitiless rapacity of the landlords. The law could not help them and, before they were utterly submerged by the landlords with every scrap of common land and vestige of liberty lost, a last stand had to be made. Heaven and earth mixed together in wars and tumults. So the Norfolk rebels published their 'complaint' so all would know the cause of their taking to arms:

THE REBELS' COMPLAINT

The pride of great men is now intolerable, but our condition miserable.

These abound in delights; and compassed with the fulness of all things and consumed with vain pleasures, thirst only after gain, inflamed with the burning delights of their desires.

But ourselves, almost killed with labour and watching, do nothing all our life long but sweat, mourn, hunger and thirst. Which things, though they seem miserable and base (as they are indeed most miserable), yet might be borne howsoever, if they which are drowned in the boiling seas of evil delights did not pursue the calamities and miseries of other men with too much insolent hatred. But now both we and our miserable condition is a laughing stock to these most proud and insolent men – who are consumed with ease and idleness. Which thing (as it may) grieveth us so sore and inflicteth such a stain of evil report, so that nothing is more grievous for us to remember, nor more unjust to suffer.

The present condition of possessing land seemeth miserable and slavish – holding it all at the pleasure of great men; not freely, but by prescription and, as it were, at the will and pleasure of the lord. For as soon as any man offend any of these gorgeous gentlemen he is put out, deprived and thrust from all his goods.

How long shall we suffer so great oppression to go unrevenged?

For so far are they, the gentlemen, now gone in cruelty and covetousness, that they are not content only to take all by violence away from us, and to consume in riot and effeminate delights what they get by force and villainy, but they must also suck in a manner our blood and marrow out of our veins and bones.

The common pastures left by our predecessors for our relief and our children are taken away.

The lands which in the memory of our fathers were common, those are ditched and hedged in and made several; the pastures are enclosed, and we shut out. Whatsoever fowls of the air or fishes of the water, and increase of the earth – all these do they devour, consume, and swallow up; yea, nature doth not suffice to satisfy their lusts, but they seek out new devices, and, as it were, forms of pleasures to embalm and perfume themselves, to abound in pleasant smells, to pour in sweet things to sweet things. Finally, they seek from all places all things for their desire and the provocation of lust. While we in the meantime eat herbs and roots, and languish with continual labour, and yet are envied that we live, breathe, and enjoy common air!

Shall they, as they have brought hedges about common pastures, enclose with their intolerable lusts also all the commodities and pleasures of this life, which Nature, the parent of us all, would have common, and bringeth forth every day, for us, as well as for them?

We can no longer bear so much, so great, and so cruel injury; neither can we with quiet minds behold so great covetousness, excess, and pride of the nobility. We will rather take arms, and mix Heaven and earth together, than endure so great cruelty.

Nature hath provided for us, as well as for them; hath given us a body and a soul, and hath not envied us other things. While we have the same form, and the same condition of birth together with them, why should they have a life so unlike unto ours, and differ so far from us in calling?

We see that things have now come to extremities, and we will prove the extremity. We will rend down the hedges, fill up ditches, and make a way for every man into the common pasture. Finally, we will lay all even with the ground, which they, no less wickedly than cruelly and covetously, have enclosed. Neither will we suffer ourselves any more to be pressed with such burdens against our wills, nor endure so great shame, since living out our days under such inconveniences we should leave the commonwealth unto our posterity – mourning, and miserable, and much worse than we received it of our fathers.

Wherefore we will try all means; neither will we ever rest until we have brought things to our own liking.

We desire liberty, and an indifferent (or equal) use of all things. This will we have. Otherwise these tumults and our lives shall only be ended together.[5]

In these plain and downright phrases the Norfolk peasants flung out their banner of revolt and called their neighbours to the fray. They did not call in vain. Kett moved his camp to nearby Eaton Wood where, on 10th July, came crowds of poor men. Word of the rising was spread throughout the county. For good or for evil, for victory or defeat, for loss or gain, the countryside was rising against the enclosures, and no man could foretell the outcome.

III

THE MARCH TO MOUSEHOLD

'This Kett was a proper person to be a ringleader of mischief. For he was of a bold, haughty spirit, and of a cankered mind against the Government.' – John Strype, *Ecclesiastical Memorials*

'The peasant, whose pigs and cow and poultry had been sold, or had died because the commons were gone where they had fed, the yeoman dispossessed of his farm, the farm servant out of employ, because where ten ploughs had turned the soil one shepherd now watched the grazing of the flocks, the artisan smarting under the famine prices which the change of culture had brought with it; all these were united in suffering, while the gentlemen were doubling, trebling, and quadrupling their incomes with their sheep farms, and adorning their persons and their houses with splendour hitherto unknown.' – J. A. Froude, *History of England*

CHAPTER III:

The March to Mousehold

Idealist and visionary, Robert Kett was a man ready for action with a clear eye to immediate necessities. A man with great qualities of generalship, able to command respect and obedience, skilful at organising and stern or kindly as occasion might demand. He was also humane, striving continually to avoid bloodshed and civil war, refusing to put his prisoners to death. Inevitably the rebels were rough and headstrong in their dealings with landowners who fell into their hands, but no savage massacre stains the annals of the rising, and the spirit of murder did not prevail.

Bowthorpe and Eaton Wood were quite unsuitable for a permanent camp, as Robert Kett's plan was to remain in arms until Somerset gave some attention to the needs of the peasantry, and definite assurance came from the Government that the wrongs of the country people would be put right. Mousehold, a wide stretch of high ground, well wooded and extending from Sprowston to Thorpe, lay to the north-east of Norwich. This was the place Kett had in mind for his headquarters.

Meanwhile, the citizens of Norwich had misgivings about the approach of the Ketts and their army. It was true that the rebels were not yet very great in number but they were a growing army; they were turbulent and wilful men, lacking proper respect for the Mayor and Corporation of the chief town in Norfolk. The citizens had direct evidence of this at Bowthorpe where the rebels immediately knocked down the fences around the Town Close, the common pastures of the city, so that all men were free to graze cattle there. This was a right which the Corporation had decided should be confined to those who paid one halfpenny a week per beast to the common herdsman. Report of what the rebels had done drove a great number of people from the city to join them.

The Mayor of Norwich, Thomas Cod, went boldly out to Bowthorpe to convince and bribe the assembly to disperse to their homes, but his efforts failed and he returned frustrated. He was important enough in his native city, but was nothing to the country people of Norfolk. He did his best to enforce his authority as chief magistrate of the city on the rebels, but it seemed impossible for the people to treat him with the seriousness he hoped for. His very name became a joke in the camp at Mousehold. Cod himself was a man of no strong character or resolution, considered harmless by his colleagues and, like other city tradesmen, he loved peace and submitted to constituted authority.

The idea of social freedom that inspired the Ketts was unintelligible to the Mayor of Norwich but he was too fearful for the property of the city to fight openly against Kett. While trying his best to get soldiers from London to suppress the rising, he remained on friendly terms with Kett and took part in the council of the leaders of the rising. Mayor Cod only showed firmness on one point – as long as it was in his power he would keep the rebels outside the city gates. Cod did all that a mayor could be expected to do for the safety of life and property but he ultimately failed to preserve the city from invasion. He also had the comforting knowledge that, on the whole, the citizens of Norwich came off better than many knights and squires in the county.

Thomas Cod, in fact, was a typical provincial mayor. His policy was to keep on good terms with the rebels whilst working to thwart their plans without incurring personal danger, until either the King's soldiers arrived to stifle the rebellion and arrest its leaders, or, should things go wrong, the rebellion become a revolution and its leaders win favour with the Government. More than once in the summer of 1549 the issue between Robert Kett and King Edward's Government must have hung in the balance, as far as Cod and the city corporation could see. It was not easy to discern the proper civic policy to be pursued under these circumstances. In the end Cod emerged from the trouble physically unharmed but broken in spirit. When things were at their hottest his public responsibilities were too heavy for his shoulders, and he passed his role on to another.

No more successful than the mayor was Sir Roger Wodehouse. This genial knight who lived at Kimberley, near Wymondham, came upon Kett's army after it had struck camp at Eaton Wood on its way to Mousehold. Sir Roger, a spirited little man, was confident that being a neighbour of the Ketts and a well-known country squire, he could get the rebels to disperse if he went about it the right way. So, he arrived at the camp with a retinue of servants and with three carts, two laden with beer and a third with provisions. The rebels were glad of the provisions and the good Norfolk ale, but when Sir Roger urged them to break up their army and turn from their unruly purpose he was jeered at for his pains, roughly handled, and after coming close to death was finally taken captive in the train of Robert Kett. He may have been short of stature but, aided by his body servant, he put up a fight, and it was not until he had been stripped of his apparel and driven into a ditch at Hellesdon Bridge, he acknowledged defeat.

That was the end of Sir Roger Wodehouse's mission. The men who had gathered round Kett were out on far too grave an errand to be diverted by a handful of money from the mayor, or a cartful of beer from Sir Roger Wodehouse. The aim of the rising was to end the enclosures or die in the process. The rebels vowed that nothing but death should turn them from their purpose, as many of them were landless and homeless and their one hope of life lay in the success of the revolt.

Kett, having decided to move his army from Eaton Wood to Mousehold as speedily as he could, sent messengers to the mayor for permission to pass through Norwich. But Mayor Cod, angered at the throwing open of the town enclosure, and annoyed at the failure of his efforts to disperse the rising, was in no mood to make concessions. His reply was a stern refusal.

Not content with this, the mayor hardly improved the occasion by lecturing the messengers on the enormity of their conduct:

He then upbraided them with many sharp and bitter checks for their disorders, as men that were seditious, and desirous of disturbing or throwing all things into confusion. He further endeavoured to deter them from their enterprise by telling them that such attempts would more surely have a bad ending, as they would soon find by experience.[1]

So the messengers returned, disappointed, to the camp. Kett was anxious to unite townsmen and peasants in a common cause, and so was in no mind for a conflict with the citizens. He decided that his army should go round via Drayton, north of the city, to reach Mousehold. The river was crossed at Hellesdon Bridge, though many passed over on trunks and branches of trees which they flung across the water. On the night of 11th July Robert Kett rested with his men at Drayton.

While Kett and his army were advancing, the Mayor and Corporation of Norwich had been sitting in solemn council, gravely discussing the situation. Some allusion to the proceedings can be found in certain items in the City Chamberlain's accounts. For instance, the sum of 40 shillings was paid to Edmund Pynchyn for his costs in riding to London and then to the King's Council in Windsor with letters concerning the rising. Nevylle reports the long and uncertain deliberations in the council chamber, particularly on the 9th and 10th of July:

Some thought no time should be lost, but that they – the rebels – should be if possible dispersed at once, since, if they were not, it was likely they would, under the influence of their excited feelings, bring ruin upon the whole country.

Others, however, thought that while the affair was one of the greatest danger, it was one that needed the most careful consideration and the most prudent counsels to bring matters to a happy termination.

'It is very true,' they said, 'that this disposition to be quick in resisting them proceeds from a high and courageous spirit; still we cannot help thinking it a rash and dangerous course to adopt – in fact, just that course, the whole praise or blame of which would depend upon the result, which at the best was doubtful, and most frequently was unfavourable. Wherefore, we advise that you fortify the city, appoint watch and ward, and dispose the citizens along the walls and in all suitable places. And since, by law, it is forbidden to collect an armed force without the King's command, we think no attempt should be made to put the rebels down, but that we ought to wait until we learn what his wishes are and receive authority from him to act.'[2]

The more cautious of the city fathers had their way on the council, falling back on the royal command against raising troops without warrant from the crown. No open hostility was displayed against Kett and no force was enrolled to dispute his authority, since to use force was illegal. All that the Corporation did was to make some attempt at fortification, to order that watch be kept, and to send messengers to the King describing the state of affairs in Norfolk.

There was considerable wisdom in not provoking Kett to battle, as the Mayor and Corporation could not rely on the inhabitants of Norwich to take united action against the rebels, and many of the town workmen had already gone over to Kett's side. But Norwich, by its passive resistance, fell under grave suspicion in London of being in league with the rebels, and many there believed the city favoured Kett's cause.

One night was spent at Drayton. On the following day Kett reached St Leonard's Hill on Mousehold, once a place of pilgrimage, where the hapless Earl of Surrey had built a house. On the road from Drayton the dovecot of John Corbet at Sprowston, which had formerly been a chapel dedicated to St Mary Magdalene, was destroyed. The keeping of pigeons had become an intolerable nuisance to the peasants, whose grain was devoured by the multitude of birds.

Having arrived at Mount Surrey, on Mousehold, the city of Norwich lay below them to the west, with the river Wensum intervening. To the south were Thorpe Wood and the village of Thorpe. The Heath itself was largely wooded, stretching north and east of the camp, three or four miles in length and breadth. It was an excellent decision to make camp on Mousehold Heath, no better site could have been found. Tragically for Kett and his army the advantage of position was lost on the fatal day of battle.

Less than a week had elapsed since the feast day at Wymondham and already Kett was encamped at Mousehold, with around 2,600 men when the first muster was called. Then, with the firing of beacons and the ringing of bells, thousands came pouring into the camp from all the homesteads and villages for miles around. In a few days no fewer than 16,000 men were enrolled under the banner of revolt. Some were vagrants, others sturdy yeomen and peasants, mostly broken and ruined men sworn to obey Kett's orders and ready to fight for the right to live. According to F. R. Russell:

The discontented, the desolate and oppressed, those for whom no man had cared, had now their 'camp', as such gatherings were called; and having this, great numbers from Norfolk, Suffolk and other parts joined them daily; blazing beacons and pealing bells spreading the tidings that the men of Norfolk had raised a standard, round which all such might gather; and far and wide was the rumour sent, and thronging multitudes came pouring in from quiet villages and market towns – the peaceful abodes of humble rustics and simple-minded farmers, hitherto content with complaining, but now roused to action as the distant beacon sent its glare across the landscape, or as the village bells, hitherto associated only with days of holy rest and happy times, forgotten now in the wild storm of social excitement in which they were living, summoned them away to join the bold spirits gathering on Mousehold Heath.[3]

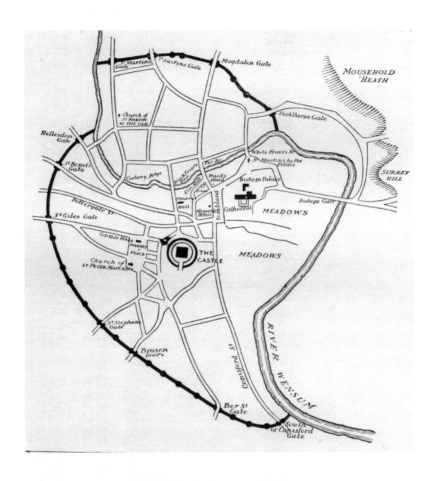

Norwich in the sixteenth century

Mousehold Heath
(etching by John Crome)

Norwich Castle
(print by Henry Ninham)

Robert Kett, under the Oak of Reformation
(print by Samuel Wale, 1778)

Bishop's Gate.
(etching by David Hodgson 1792)

St Stephen's Gate
(print by Walter Halgreen)

Avg Steward

Mayor 1534
1546
1556

Augustine Steward, Mayor of Norwich

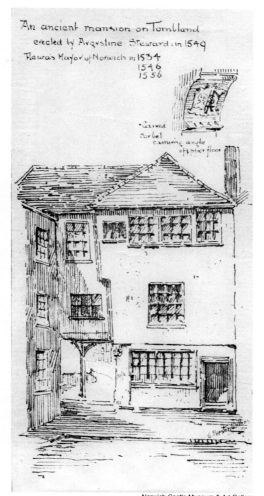

An ancient mansion on Tombland
erected by Augustine Steward in 1549
He was Mayor of Norwich in 1534
1546
1556

Carved
corbel
carrying angle
of upper floor

Augustine Steward's house in Tombland

Wymondham Abbey
(print by John Cotman)

IV

THE OAK OF REFORMATION

'Twenty thousand men gathered round the "Oak of Reformation" near Norwich, and repulsing the royal troops in a desperate engagement, renewed the old cries for a removal of evil counsellors, a prohibition of enclosures, and redress for the grievances of the poor.'
J. R. Green, *History of England*

'These villains were so far from a due sense of their wickedness in plundering, imprisoning and abusing their honest neighbours and disturbing the public tranquillity, that they had a chaplain, Conyers, Vicar of St Martin's, Norwich, to say morning and evening service and pray to God to prosper their ungodly enterprise.' Oldmixon, *History of the Reign of Edward VI*

CHAPTER IV:

The Oak of Reformation

Having led his army to Mousehold, Kett was to show the kind of man he was, and what qualities of generalship he possessed. It was one thing to lead 20,000 homeless, hungry men in revolt, to Mousehold Heath but he was to direct these stormy elements and carry out a definite policy of social change.

Plainly, Robert Kett was no mere demagogue. He was far more than a popular agitator, or the mouthpiece of revolt. He had very positive and definite views of the work in hand, and at Mousehold he immediately set about the fulfilment of his plans. On one thing he was determined – that the people of Norfolk should have justice and an end to their present miseries. Kett sent off a petition to the King and set his camp in order at Mousehold, believing that Protector Somerset was in earnest about stopping the enclosures and that the Government meant to deal fairly by the people. Two things were necessary: discipline in the rebel army, and an adequate supply of arms and provisions. Despite difficulties, Kett successfully accomplished both in the six weeks he held command. More than that, he disempowered the landlords and curbed all seizures of the common fields.

Kett would not admit that he was a rebel. He insisted that this work was not rebellion but loyalty to the commonwealth of England, to free the country from the lawless power of the landowners. In Kett's view the rising was not a wanton act of riot, but a serious and responsible movement, with every semblance of law and order. Providing food for the army at Mousehold was done on Kett's authority through a levy on the landowners, whose actions were the cause of all the troubles.

Under a famous tree at Mousehold, called from that time the 'Oak of Reformation', Robert Kett issued orders daily and administered justice.[1] With him were associated William Kett and three reputable citizens of Norwich: Thomas Cod, the mayor; Thomas Aldrich, an elderly alderman, considered wise, honest, and for whom there was a lot of affection; and Robert Watson, a well regarded new preacher. These three were obliged to join Kett, not because they agreed with the revolt, but because they hoped to curb the rebels' behaviour and prevent an attack on the city. Watson was a persuasive person and, with Aldrich, often preserved the peace between Cod and Kett.[2] For all their efforts Cod, Aldrich, and Watson could not prevent Kett from arresting and fining landowners, and destroying their enclosures. They thought it safer to consent to what they were powerless to stop.

In addition to the three townsmen, Kett ordered that two men be chosen from each of the hundreds in the county to assist the tribunal at the Oak of Reformation. The names of these deputies were published at the head of the 'Requests and Demands' petition which Kett sent to the King.[3]

This Bill of 'Requests and Demands' was signed by Kett, Cod and Aldrich, and contained the full grievances of the country folk. It was a lengthy document and the petitions included the preservation of the common fields, the establishment of fair rents, the restoration of fishing rights, the appointment of resident clergymen in every parish to preach and instruct the children, and the recognition of locally elected commissioners with powers to enforce the laws. One significant request was 'that all bondmen may be made free, for God made all free with his precious bloodshedding.'

The 'Requests and Demands' were moderate and free from all revolutionary sentiment. They reveal a wide and detailed knowledge of the various hardships of the country people, and explain a lot of the unrest of the time. They show that Kett had a very clear understanding of the immediate and practical reforms that were needed in the county of Norfolk.

The King was quick but evasive in his reply to the Bill of 'Requests and Demands.' According to Haywood he was offended to be treated as if he was the enemy, and Kett's men lawful.[4] Somerset listed in this reply what had been done to put things right; the proclamation against excessive food prices, and commissioners appointed for the reformation of enclosures and also to see the reduction of rents and wool prices. In addition, four or six representatives of the county were to be allowed to present their grievances to Parliament in October. In the meantime, the Protector claimed, these disorders had delayed his plans. He asked the people to get on with their usual duties, especially the harvest, as he did not want to use sharper means to keep order.[5]

This reply, with a general pardon, was brought to Mousehold by a herald. 'Herewith also the King sent his general pardon, in case they would quietly desist and dissolve; but it was all, unhappily, of no avail.'[6]

How could the homeless and landless peasants of East Anglia apply themselves to harvest and other peaceable business at home? What hope was there for this long-suffering multitude in the promise that Parliament would meet to look into their grievances some months later? Year after year the people had waited for help while their condition went steadily from bad to worse, their old rights and liberties vanishing before the advancing wave of landlord aggression. Something more definite than this royal reply was required to make them disperse, as they had now found a leader whom they trusted. If there was to be no assistance from the King's Government in London, then Kett's army would have to fight for freedom.

This answer to his petition left Robert Kett unmoved. When Parliament met and fulfilled these pledges it would be time for him to resign his charge, but to give up the work now would be sheer folly. Over and over again the people had been fooled by royal promises, such as those of Richard II at the time of the great uprising in 1381. Neither did the Crown keep the promises it gave to the commons of Kent, when Jack Cade led them to London in 1450. If Protector Somerset were in earnest to help the people recover their rights, his task should be aided, not impeded, by the resolute action of the people striving for their rights. Popular indifference and a return to abject submission would provide Parliament with a fatal excuse for doing nothing, and would probably bring down heavy vengeance on the heads of all who had dared revolt.

To Robert Kett the path of duty was plain and unmistakable. He had pledged his word not to lay down his command until the rights of his poorer neighbours had been won. He had vowed to spend not only his substance, but his very life in the cause in which they had all embarked. Justice must be done in Norfolk, whatever King or Parliament decided, and it should be done in the name of King and Commonwealth. It might be that if this one corner of England were cleansed of oppression, the fire of social regeneration would spread to other parts. Already there was news of the people rising in the counties of Buckingham, Oxford, Surrey, Essex, Kent and Cambridge.

So Kett proceeded to do justice and to order his plan of campaign beneath the Oak of Reformation. It was an old oak with great spread boughs, and over these boughs they laid rafters and cross beams, and made a roof with boards. To feed the camp Kett issued a warrant in his own name, and in the name of the deputies elected by the hundreds of Norfolk:

> We, the King's Friends and Delegates, give authority to all men for the searching out of   beasts and all kind of victual, to be brought into the camp at Mousehold wheresoever they find it, so that no violence or injury be done to any honest or poor man: charging all men by the authority hereof that as they wish well unto the King and the afflicted commonwealth they be obedient to us his Delegates and unto them whose names are written below.[7]

Bodies of men armed with these warrants were sent out to the country houses in different parts of the county. They returned with money, cattle and corn, and with guns and gunpowder. No resistance was made to these demands by the terrified landowners, and no lives were taken. The smaller farmers offered Kett's men provisions with a great deal of goodwill.

To prevent personal thefts, the people were strictly warned against robbing and spoiling, and were required to make their account at the Oak of Reformation. If those who had concealed any goods obtained by Kett's warrants were discovered, and the crime proved, they were at once sent to prison. It was inevitable that some of the goods were not handed over to the common store, but every case of private plunder that was found was tried at the Oak, and every offender convicted of theft was punished.

After this the rebels began to arrest those landowners who had made enclosures and many of the county gentry fled for their lives. The citizens of Norwich became anxious at the tales of the open comandeering of property, and were only kept from a violent panic by the knowledge that Cod, Aldrich, and Watson were in daily conference with the rebel leaders at Mousehold. Kett sent word to these citizens:

> We are the King's friends, and being unjustly oppressed, we have taken upon ourselves the defence of the laws and of the King's Majesty.

In order to maintain better discipline and order among the rebels, Kett seized the opportunity of giving some of his followers the authority of magistrates. A royal messenger had been sent to deliver commissions of the peace to various county gentlemen, giving them the power to keep order. However, he fell into the hands of Kett's men, who at once took these documents and sent him on his way. Kett then filled in the commissions with the names of certain trustworthy men whom he picked out, and these new magistrates co-operated with the delegates of the hundreds in maintaining order.

The Oak of Reformation was not only Kett's court of justice, it was also a place of prayer and preaching. Dr Conyers, vicar of St

Martin's at the palace in Norwich, was the chaplain to the camp. He read the prayers of the new Book of Common Prayer daily to whoever attended, and other clergymen were able to come out from the city without hindrance and preach under the Oak. No objection was taken when Mayor Cod and old Master Aldrich ascended this pulpit from time to time and endeavoured to discourage the rebels from violent courses of action. In fact, Kett allowed the full use of the Oak to any of the Norwich citizens who wished to address his followers. But the preaching and remonstrances gained no sympathetic hearing.

On one occasion Dr Matthew Parker, formerly chaplain to Henry VIII and Anne Boleyn, came to the camp at Mousehold. He had been born and bred in Norwich and visited with his brother, Thomas Parker, who was later Mayor of Norwich in 1568. It was evening when they came, and a discussion was going on between Kett and Cod. Kett was urging the Mayor to resign his office, or at least to give up the keys of the city, but Cod replied that he would sooner lay down his life than desert the city or fail in his duty to the King.

Parker's purpose was to preach to the rebels, but he found everybody more interested in the question of Cod's resignation. A great deal of eating and drinking had also taken place that day in the camp (it was said that no less than 3,000 bullocks and 20,000 sheep, besides swans, geese, hens and ducks, had been already devoured in a week at Mousehold!). The people were also tired and hot, so no one wanted to listen to Dr Parker that night. Parker was disgusted that the common people were drunk, and put his sermon off to the following day as he was determined to preach it.

Whatever may have been their condition that night, the people were all at prayers when Parker appeared to fulfil his mission in the morning. So the doctor went up into the Oak and began his sermon by lecturing the rebels on their intemperance. He was shocked at the extravagance and luxury he had seen, and believed this behaviour to be wicked. The preacher's second point was that no private feuds should be avenged, no blood shed, and no man's life be taken. Even those they held as enemies should not to be imprisoned or kept in bonds. In the third place, the people were exhorted to stop their enterprise and trust the heralds and messengers of the King. Then followed a glowing eulogy on the King and the importance of postponing their demands until the King was of age:

> Let them give unto the King due honour, even in his young and tender age, whereby they might use him hereafter, when he came to more ripe and flourishing estate.[8]

The people had listened attentively enough at the beginning, but Parker's admonitions were too much for them and angry interruptions broke the thread of the discourse. Someone shouted out that the preacher was in the pay of the landlords, and the cry was taken up:

> How long shall we bear with this hireling doctor? He's hired by the gentry, and so he comes with words for which they have paid him, and with his tongue bribed by them.

That was the end of the sermon, for the people would stand no more of this kind of preaching. Things began to look awkward for the preacher, and there were even threats of shooting at him with pikes and arrows unless he came down from the tree. Some bold and impudent spirits actually pretended to prick the soles of his feet with their spears. Parker became exceedingly afraid at this, but there was no real danger. Chaplain Conyers soon restored peace to his excited congregation when, with three or four choristers, he began to sing the *Te Deum* in English.[9]

Parker came down from the tree while the singing held the attention of the people, and left with his brother. However, he was not allowed to make his way home entirely unmolested. Going down the hill toward Pockthorpe Gate a number of the rebels overtook Parker and began to question him as to whether he had a licence to preach from the Crown, asking to see the great seal on his licence. While his brother Thomas held them in conversation, Matthew Parker managed to escape quietly and so reached the city unhurt.[10]

With Parker's visit over, the first week of Kett's camp at Mousehold was ended. Robert Kett sat daily at the Oak to do justice while his men scoured the country for arms and provisions, and brought in landowners to be judged.

Kett was still anxious that the citizens of Norwich should take an active part in the rising. He continued to press the mayor to give up the keys of the city gates, but Cod declined to do this on any terms. Kett, on his side, was determined to avoid an open quarrel with the mayor and trusted in time to bring the citizens over to the side of the peasants. His policy all along was a united Norfolk – townsmen and country folk combined against all who held with the landlords.

Nevertheless, conflict soon raged between the city and the rebel peasants.

V

THE CONFLICT WITH THE CITIZENS

'Apart from the recovery of what the peasants thought was stolen property, their conduct was restrained and almost orderly. Rude courts were held by Kett and his reluctant assessor, the Mayor of Norwich, in the rebels' camp; and if the justice they administered was rough, it was probably as fair as that obtainable in the King's courts, where, according to the proverb of that day the law was ended as a man was friended.' – A. F. Pollard, *Political History*

CHAPTER V:

The Conflict with the Citizens

Kett was mistaken to count on sympathy for the rising from the city. It was true that a certain number of town labourers and artisans joined the rebel army, but the wealthy citizens of Norwich were always hostile to the movement. The turbulent actions of the rebels were a hindrance to trade, and the camp at Mousehold was a constant menace to the peace of the city. Without doubt the fact that Mayor Cod, old Alderman Aldrich, and the persuasive preacher Watson were with Kett was reassuring to timid minds. As yet no real injury had been done to life and property within the city, but who could tell how long it would be before things changed for the worse?

Every day brought news of fresh aggression on the part of the rebels. It was all too evident that they were utterly without respect for the county gentry and had no reverence for learning. Dr Matthew Parker, the eminent divine and distinguished master of Corpus Christi College, Cambridge, a man who had been a Queen's chaplain and of whom all Norwich was proud, had actually been ignominiously derided by these unruly followers of Robert Kett. More than that, not content with seizing cattle and demanding arms and provisions everywhere, the peasants were arresting the gentlefolk, bringing them to the Oak on Mousehold to be tried as common offenders before Kett, and hauling them to prison in the city and at St Leonard's Hill. Such high-handed proceedings were naturally a shock to the tradesmen of Norwich.

There was also irritation at the spectacle of the rebels coming in and going out of the city every day as they pleased. The city authorities had no force at their disposal to keep them out, and were still afraid of breaking the law which forbade taking up arms without the permission of the Crown. All that the mayor could do was to retain the keys of the city gates. Against his will the mayor supplied the rebels with funds, when Kett insisted that the city must grant him money, since the work being done by the army on Mousehold was in defence of the liberties of the county.

Mayor Cod's position was extremely difficult. For the sake of the city he was constrained to keep on good terms with Kett, and up to now no rioting had taken place within the walls. However, it was hard for Cod to have to show civility to a pack of rebels and traitors. Kett trusted in time to bring all Norwich on his side, and likewise Cod trusted in time to bring troops from London and end the rising. Both Kett and Cod kept an outward show of peace between the camp and the city, until the relations were strained to breaking point exactly nine days after the arrival at Mousehold. An unsuccessful mission by York Herald was the direct cause of the rupture.

The city fathers had despatched a messenger to London at the outset of Kett's march, and again directly after Matthew Parker's visit. This second envoy was Leonard Sotherton, a respectable burgess, who went off to London on his own account to report to the King's Council and beg for help.

Sotherton was summoned before the Council to tell his story, and explained that the uprising had threatened to destroy the city and all the gentry. However, rather that send soldiers to Norwich, he suggested the proclamation of a royal pardon, in the hope that such an offer would cause a large number of the rebels to return to their homes as 'faithful and true subjects are wont to do.'[1] This advice seemed an easy way for the Royal Council, who had their hands fully engaged in other ways, to end the disturbance. York Herald was sent off with Sotherton to Norwich, arriving at midday on 21st July.

Meanwhile, Cod and Aldrich had been protesting strongly to Kett against the arrest and imprisonment of the landowners, some of whom were being held in Norwich Prison (at the Guildhall), some in Norwich Castle and some in Surrey place. Kett, convinced this was justice, was unmoved by the admonitions of the mayor, and the rebels generally rejoiced at the downfall of those who, they said. 'had sought by all ways to oppress them'.

Conscious that their own words carried no weight at Mousehold, the mayor and his colleagues now looked to the King's herald to have some influence with the rebels. Accordingly, on the arrival of York Herald they immediately approached the Oak.

York Herald was received with cheers on his approach to the camp, and the assembly listened attentively while he read the King's pardon to all who would give up the rebellion and depart quietly back to their house. But the herald was not content with declaring a general pardon, he went on to trounce Kett and all his company for their misdeeds. He expanded his official message and threatened 'all severity of punishment' for those who remained in arms:

Hearken all you that be here, and thou, Kett, captain of mischief, and as many of you as are present, give ear. Although the manner of our ancestors, and the dignity of this empire, and the majesty of the name of a King seem to require, that you, which have wickedly taken upon you arms against your country, and have cast yourselves into open conspiracy and rebellion, having been put to flight by sword and fire, should receive due punishment for the wickedness which you have committed: yet notwithstanding, so great is the kindness and clemency of the King's Majesty, that those whose heinous offence craveth for condign punishment, of his singular and incredible favour, he will have preserved with safety. And therefore commandeth that, forthwith, every man lay down his arms: that they forsake the camp and this den of thieves, and everyone to depart to his own house. And if you have done this thing, being deceived, ye have your pardon, and warrant of impunity of all the evils ye have done: but if ye shall remain in your former mind and purpose of wickedness, he will surely revenge all the hurts and villainies that you have done, as is meet, and with all severity of punishment. Neither will he suffer any longer to remain, to the overthrow of the whole kingdom, the things that are to be cut off and cannot be healed.

For a moment the people standing around the herald were moved by these words. Some shouted 'God save the King's Majesty!' and others 'on their knees fell down giving God and the King's Majesty great thanks for his gracious clemency and pity.'[2]

But to Kett all this talk of pardon and this berating of them, as though they were disobedient schoolboys, was beside the point. He waited for an assurance from the Crown that some immediate check would be placed on the tyranny of the landowners, and that justice would be enforced between landlord and tenant. This message of this herald was no better than the message of the previous herald. In neither case was any definite reply given to the Bill of 'Requests and Demands'. The grievances were not redressed, and it was to remedy these grievances that Kett and his company had taken up arms. To give up their camp and disband the army would leave Norfolk to anarchy, as at least some method and order had been established at Mousehold. Moreover, in openly striking a blow against landlord rule, Kett could not admit that he or his followers had done wrong, rather they were taking steps to end the wrong. Impatiently, but not without dignity, Robert Kett answered the herald:

Kings and princes are wont to pardon wicked persons, not innocent and just men. We, for our part, have deserved nothing and are guilty to ourselves of no crime; and, therefore, we despise such speeches as idle and unprofitable to our business. I trust I have done nothing but what belongs to the duty of a true subject.

Kett then turned his attention to the body of men gathered before him and said a few words to reassure them of his purpose, and encourage their loyalty to their leader, as he had little chance of a pardon. At this speech the people cheered heartily for their captain and it was plain the herald's errand had failed.

The herald was indignant at the answer he had received and denounced the rebels as traitors, calling upon John Petibone, the sword-bearer of Norwich, to arrest Robert Kett. But to do this was manifestly beyond the city sword-bearer's power, and the word 'arrest' provoked a stirring among the rebels. John Petibone was more than willing to obey the herald's command, but how could he and half-a-dozen elderly members of the Town Council, armed only with slight authority, arrest Robert Kett, supported by 20,000 desperate fellows? The task was impossible, Kett must be left to his own devices.

Mayor Cod, Alderman Aldrich, Swordbearer Petibone and the rest of the city fathers who had come to Mousehold, escorted the herald back to Norwich. They were followed by a number of the rebels who professed repentance.

Once within the city, Cod ordered the city gates to be made fast, and on the advice of his colleagues and citizens, good watch to be kept. Then the gentry, imprisoned within the city by Kett, were set free and invited to join the Mayor's council of war. However, no sooner were these prisoners released than it was discovered that many of Kett's men were in the city, so it was decided that the gentlemen should be shut up in the Castle again, in case the rebels should come across them and murder them.

Were ever English county gentlemen so beset with fear as these poor, cowardly landowners of Norfolk? With the exception of the fierce little Sir Roger Woodhouse, who remained Kett's prisoner, not a single landowner around Norwich showed fight or even protested during the whole time of the rising. Although in other parts of the county there were both spirited and successful attacks on the rebels.

With Norwich more or less under arms, anticipating a visit from Kett, all peace between the camp and the citizens was now at an end. Ten of the largest cannons in the city were posted on the castle ditches, and Kett pointed his guns from the hill overlooking Norwich. Firing commenced on the evening of 21st July and, commented Wood, 'the whole night was spent in fearful shot on both sides'. However, this 'fearful shot' did little injury as the distance on either side was too great for the range of the guns. Kett's cannon-balls brought more fear than damage to the city, and the city ordnance had little effect on the enemy.[3]

In the morning the citizens moved their ordnance in to the meadows by the river on the east of the city, and Kett had his cannon brought to the bottom of the hill.

A last attempt at peace was made by Kett before the firing was renewed. Two envoys, Isaac Williams, a tailor, and Ralph Sutton, a hatter, came from the camp at Mousehold to the mayor, bearing a flag of truce. They requested restoration of the right of way through the city so that provisions could be brought to the camp. Unless this free passage was restored, and a truce made for at least a few days, the passage would be forced and death and destruction dealt to the city.[4]

Mayor Cod's reply to this threatening request was an uncompromising refusal, as the mayor was not without courage while he held command in the city. According to Nevylle, the mayor made a long speech, and replied to the envoys as follows:

They were the most wretched traitors, guilty of all disloyalty and of unheard-of villainy. He would not, therefore, grant anything to their most iniquitous demands; nor, if he were willing, was it allowable to do so, especially as they were the most abandoned of men. That they had committed so many, and such intolerable, villainies as to deserve being not only shut out of the city, but also, if it were possible, thrust only beyond the pale of human nature itself. That they despised the King's Majesty, wasted the country, almost utterly destroyed the city of Norwich, had branded upon themselves and their posterity an everlasting mark of reproach for villainy and treason, and that all parts had by their violence and crimes been harassed, polluted, troubled and laid waste. And yet you ask to be admitted into the city? To enjoy the rights of citizens? To share in their civil and religious privileges? To have your want of food relieved by them? What? Do you not repent of the crimes of which you have been guilty? Are you not, at the very least, ashamed of them? Verily, I know not whether they who have committed such acts are the more wicked, or they who made this request are the more shameless? Do you hope to obtain them from the Mayor? From whom lately you made to suffer the shame and disgrace of imprisonment? Do you hope to obtain them from this city? Have you not almost utterly destroyed it, and can you think it will help you now? But perhaps you think the citizens will aid you? Just consider how you have treated them: have you not brought war upon them, with all its horrors; and do you suppose that they will supply you with corn and provisions to serve as food for your fury? What folly to entertain such hopes! Be off then, be off, and tell Kett, the leader of these abominable conspirators, that the citizens of Norwich will obey the King's Majesty and not these traitors, wretches that no longer deserve the name of men; while, as regards myself, I think nothing of the dangers and horrors you are preparing against the city. Break in, lay waste, destroy, cut down and overthrow, just as you please; but remember that God is the avenger and punisher of all such doings, and that sooner or later your consciences will prick you for the great crimes you have been guilty of – and remember also, that you will undoubtedly, and at no distant period, meet with the punishment you have by your madness and folly drawn upon yourselves.[5]

On learning of the mayor's refusal, Kett immediately decided to force a passage and ordered the guns to be fired. The city fired from the other side of the river but the gunners lacked powder and skill, and the reply was of little use. Artillery proved useless, so bows and arrows became the chief weapons of war inside and outside the city. The inadequacy of the gunners was more than made up for by the desperate bravery of the invaders.

First the rebels tried to storm the gates at Bishopsgate, Pockthorpe, and Magdalen Gate. With loud outcries they rushed down the hill upon the city, but the charge was withstood, especially by bowmen. The rebels continued their attack despite being shot at with a great number of arrows:

> So impudent were they and so desperate, that their vagabond boys, naked and unarmed, came among the thickest of the arrows and gathered them up, when some of the said arrows stuck fast in their legs and other parts...[they] plucked out the very arrows that were sticking in their bodies, and gave them, all dripping with blood, to the rebels who were standing round to fire again at the city, and this utter contempt of danger and weakness so dismayed the archers (within the city) that it took their heart from them.[6]

By noon an entry had been forced at Bishopsgate, as the rebels swam the river and took the city gunner by surprise. Greatly outnumbered and short of both powder and skill with a cannon, he abandoned his station and fled. The citizens all began to flee from the gates and walls and the rebels were quickly masters of the city. Kett's friends within Norwich certainly hastened the victory, and all the next morning there were cries throughout the city: 'To arms, to arms, citizens, the enemy are within the walls.' The City Chamberlain's Accounts also mention that on 22nd July about eighty of Kett's men took gunpowder and pikes from the chamberlain's house.

It does not appear that any great loss of life occurred during the seizure of Norwich by the rebels, or that the citizens suffered any harm to their property. It was ten days later, after the defeat of Lord Northampton, when the real miseries fell upon the city.

Nevertheless, York Herald could not bear to leave Kett in authority, and was moved to make a final appeal to the rebels to disperse.

Accompanied by the mayor, many important citizens and a large crowd of people, the herald went into the market-place and solemnly repeated the warnings and promises of the previous day. Once more he ordered them to lay down their arms, leave the camp, depart to their own homes, and rely on the mercy and pity of the King. If they would do this then they should be safe and free from fear of punishment. However, if they remained in arms they had nothing to expect but 'grievous torments, bitter death, and all extremity'.

The rebels had grown impatient of threats and preaching and were excited at the victory they had won. To the great astonishment of the herald the crowd shouted and howled all the way to the Market Cross, as though they had already won. The appeal of the herald was heard with open contempt, he was told to leave and there was none of the previous day's inclination to listen to the promises of a pardon:

> Depart with a plague on thee! cried the rebels. To the devil with these idle promises. He must be mad to think to get round us with fine speeches, so as to bring us to ruin. We shall only be oppressed in the end. We detest such mercy which, under pretence of pardon, would cut off all hope of safety and self-preservation.[7]

After this the herald did leave, not with a plague, but with eight good pieces of gold (£4) in his pocket, which the Corporation paid him. Alderman Steward and others of the city fathers escorted York Herald to St Stephen's Gate where, at the herald's request, they left him to ride to London alone, while the rebels continued shouting in the streets.

With the herald gone and the free passage of provisions through the city secured by the rebels, Kett went back to Mousehold. To prevent any further opposition from the city fathers he also insisted that many of the most important citizens be brought to the camp. There they were held in chains at Surrey place, and Sotherton reported that some even died. The names of those in chains, or who died, are not known. Thomas Aldrich was clearly at large all this time and the mayor was soon released.[8]

By the close of day on 22nd July Mayor Cod was deeply humiliated. In the morning he had defied Kett; in the evening he was a prisoner, in bonds at Mousehold, no longer an authority in the city nor a person of importance in the rebel camp. He was greeted with jeers and derision and his life was threatened. Men ridiculed his name and cried out in imitation of the herald's pompous style:

Oyes! Oyes! As many as will come to the camp tomorrow shall buy a cod's head for a penny.

All this boisterousness was shocking to the townsfolk and it seemed shameful that these ill-mannered, disreputable peasants should mock the Chief Magistrate of Norwich. It was also reported that the mayor's life was in danger, so a group of citizens went to Alderman Aldrich to urge him to move on behalf of their mayor.

The old alderman was popular with the rebels, Kett always treated him with great respect and no man in Norwich had more influence at the camp than Aldrich, whose ideas and advice were taken seriously. On more than one occasion he had succeeded in returning goods taken by the rebels, and in restraining Kett's followers from some of their proposals.

Alderman Aldrich went without hesitation and told Kett that Cod must be released, asking him how he dared to imprison a man who was not only harmless, but a Mayor? Kett did not answer at once, but sat fixed in thought. As the old alderman insisted, Kett consented, and Cod was immediately taken from confinement, and given liberty to come and go as before.

But the spirit of the mayor was broken and his glory was departed. He was rather glad to be at the camp, as near Kett he felt safe at least from personal injury. He had failed to keep the rebels away from the city and could no longer exert his authority. So Thomas Cod resigned as mayor and appointed Alderman Austen Steward, who lived in Tombland (in the big house exactly opposite Erpingham Gate) to be his deputy. Alderman Henry Bacon and John Atkinson were appointed as sheriffs. Between them these three men kept all but the worst of the citizens peaceful.

After this, Thomas Cod was merely a shadow of his former self. He had once walked proudly amongst his fellow-citizens, conscious of their approval, but was to become a nobody. His person and goods were safe, as he lived unmolested at Mousehold, but the pride of the chief magistrate was humbled to the dust. It was a hard task to be a mayor amidst these turmoils and commotions.[9]

Meanwhile there was much for Kett to do. His army of 20,000 still needed to be fed, and he was anxious that the movement he was leading should spread. It was all very well to have broken down the enclosures in that corner of Norfolk, but his mind was set on more than a local revolt. His desire was to save England from the landowners, if such a task was possible.

Kett remained under the Oak of Reformation at his old work, while envoys were sent out on all sides to rouse the country, as missionaries of social revolution carrying news of the work at Norwich. Under the oak he administered justice and ensured that law and order was maintained within the ranks of his followers. This was no easy task as the men had been long oppressed and did not find it easy, in the first days of freedom, to submit willingly to rule. But Kett's authority was supreme. The people believed in their leader, trusted him implicitly and obeyed orders.

The campaign against the landowners continued. Nevylle reported:

The rebels cried out against the gentlemen, not only for that they would not pull down their enclosed grounds, but also because they understood by letters found among their

71

servants how they sought by all ways to oppress them: and whatsoever might be said they would have down with the gentlemen. So that within two or three weeks they had so pursued the gentlemen from all parts that in no place durst one keep to his house, but were fain to spoil themselves of their apparel and lie and keep in woods and sheltered places where no resort was. Some fled out of the country and glad were others in their houses to save the rest of their goods and cattle by providing daily bread, meat, drink and all other viands, and by carrying the same at their own charge to the rebels' camp – for the saving of their wives, children and servants.

At that time it must have seemed to the country people that the power of the landlords was broken. These landlords had taken away the very means of life from the peasants and ridden roughshod over the law, but now they were shamed and either in hiding, in flight, in service to the camp, or in prison at the Guildhall, Norwich Castle or Surrey place.[10]

Although the condition of the landlords was poor, it should be remembered that in every case their lives were spared. Kett was not a man of blood, and it was not his intention to provoke civil war, or leave a legacy of hatred by putting his neighbours to death. He was always mindful of his goal to end the oppression of the people by breaking the power of the landowners. Kett laboured for that purpose and neither faltered nor turned from the path he had chosen. He believed that he was called to deliver his poorer neighbours from their evil plight, hoping that this rising in Norfolk might be the beginning of a national movement. Kett acted with resolution from the day he accepted the responsibility of leadership at Wymondham, but he would not permit the taking of human life if Norfolk could attain freedom by other methods. In the battle and hard fighting to come Kett was to prove himself a skilful soldier, ready to kill or be killed if necessary. In his dealings with the county landlords he was the judge, stern and unmoved by any respect of persons, and without the shadow of cruelty, meanness or thirst for blood.

Day after day the landowners who had been arrested for making enclosures were brought before Kett at the Oak, to answer for their offences against the common good. When nothing was proved against the prisoner the people would cry, 'He is a good man; a good man,' and the defendant would be promptly set free. If any small crime or offence was known, the cry went up, 'Let him be hanged; let him be hanged', and when the prisoner asked why he should be hanged, the people would answer that 'Others had used such words against them, and, therefore, they would use these same words again.'[11] Often a vagrant or homeless peasant had been condemned to the gallows for no offence but homelessness. Now the peasants, whose sons and brothers were so ruthlessly dealt with for the crime of poverty, wanted to set the hangman to work on their executioners.

The long pent-up hatred against 'the gentlemen' who had depopulated the countryside, flamed the calling for revenge. These men had demolished whole villages, broken up the common fields and caused hard-working folk to starve, beg, steal, and die in slavery or on the gallows, all because pasturage was more profitable to the landlord than tillage.

To them, no other reason for capital punishment was needed but that Kett's prisoners were gentlemen, and therefore not worthy to live. If Robert Kett had been a weaker man he would have yielded to the clamour for blood. Had he been less humane, or an implacable and inflexible tyrant, he would have ordered the destroyers of rural England to summary execution. The landlords were in his control, Kett only needed to say the word and they would die, just as they had caused the death of so many others.

Kett never gave the order, and the landlords were not hanged. It was no 'bloody assize' at the Oak of Reformation. Robert Kett could show the judges and lawmakers of England that the people in power were more merciful than their rulers, that democracy and social equality could not to be set up by the hangman.

Kett may have discerned that these landlords were not so guilty as they appeared. They merely followed the instinct to grow rich and powerful; their fault was in their lack of feeling. It was the system, that allowed a few to possess the land and oppress their fellow men, that was wrong and had to be overthrown. In time, these landlords, now trembling before him for their lives, might learn from it. Dispossessed of their unrighteous power, a fuller and better life could be theirs in social service and mutual aid with their neighbours. It might be, too, that in receiving mercy, the prejudice of their class would yield and they would come to believe that the camp at Mousehold was noble and worthy of the support of all true and good men. They were Englishmen, just as he was, so why should they not join hands together? By sparing his prisoners Kett could reasonably hope to influence other landowners to view the rising favourably. Feelings of humanity and good generalship argued against putting the landlords to death.

However, the landlords did not raise their voices for a pardon for the peasants when, a few weeks later, their cause was lost. When their hour of peril had passed, the Norfolk squires expressed no gratitude for the mercy they had received. The insults and injuries they had suffered sat too deeply in their hearts to make such a thing possible. They had been imprisoned as common criminals, robbed and their goods destroyed, and felt no gratitude because their lives were not taken.

Trade was at an end in Norwich in those last days of July 1549, and there was considerable unrest in the city. But Steward, the deputy mayor, and the sheriffs had Kett's authority to maintain order. By this time, as Steward admitted, a large number of citizens sided with the rebels.

On 29th July word was brought to Kett that Lord Northampton was marching from London with a body of troops to end the rising. And, sure enough, two days later Northampton was seen at the city gates.

So this was the answer of Somerset's Government to the 'Requests and Demands' of Robert Kett and his company. And now it had come to pass that the men of Mousehold Camp must fight hard, even to the death, if they were not to be overcome in their mission.

VI

THE DEFEAT OF LORD NORTHAMPTON

'The Marquis being thus beaten out of Norwich, with the residue that escaped, hasted to London, leaving the city in the rebels' power; many of the chief citizens fled, leaving their wives, children and all their possessions in their enemies' hands.' – Blomefield, *History of Norfolk*

CHAPTER VI:

The Defeat of Lord Northampton

When the York Herald returned to London, the Royal Council immediately sent a force to Norwich to suppress the rebels. William Parr, Marquis of Northampton, was in command of the expedition, and arrived within a mile of the city on the afternoon of 31st July. With him were Lord Sheffield and Lord Wentworth, a number of knights and country squires with their retainers, and about 1,500 soldiers, including a body of Italian mercenaries.

A herald, Norroy, King-at-Arms, was sent to summon the city to submit, or war would be declared. Alderman Steward immediately replied that Thomas Cod, the mayor, was a prisoner in Kett's camp, but that he would be contacted to decide if Lord Northampton should be admitted. On receiving his deputy's message Cod made a characteristic reply, as his confinement at Mousehold did not hinder free expression of opinion. He urgently advised the surrender of the city to Northampton. Cod apologised for the state of things in Norwich and regretted that he was kept from welcoming the Marquis; he would have come at once had Kett permitted it.

Steward agreed with Cod entirely concerning the propriety of welcoming Northampton and his soldiers into the city. And so, accompanied by a large number of citizens, he set out to meet Northampton. He took with him the Sword of State, the symbol of the King's authority, which in the chief cities of England was always carried before the mayor.

Steward explained to Northampton the regrettable but unavoidable absence of Mayor Cod and promised, on behalf of the loyal citizens, ready and willing obedience to the King's commands.

The deputy mayor declared that he and the chief of the city had come to hand authority over the city to the King. They confessed there were many citizens who had sided with the rebels, but that the greatest number had, in no way, conspired against the King's Majesty. Those present were ready and willing to do whatever was required of them. In return, Northampton promised to protect the loyal citizens, and added that he hoped to put down the rebellion very quickly.

The mayor's Sword of State was then delivered to Sir Richard Southwell who, bareheaded, carried it before the Marquis of Northampton. A procession was formed and St Stephen's Gate was thrown open, allowing the city to be entered with due solemnity. The Marquis was at once taken to the Council Chamber and refreshed with 'bread, drink, meat, wine, fruit and other things'.

The next move was to the market-place where a great crowd assembled, and a long discussion took place between Northampton and the principal citizens. It was decided that the city should be carefully defended against any attack from the camp at Mousehold, and men were appointed to keep strict watch. Northampton, who was nothing of a soldier, went off with his knights to eat and sleep in Steward's big house in Tombland.

The fighting began that same evening, due to a party of the Italian mercenaries who had strayed beyond the gates. They encountered a number of Kett's men on Magdalen Hill and were driven back with some losses. An Italian nobleman was amongst the prisoners taken, and he was hanged without mercy on Mount Surrey, although many, it was said, 'would have given as much as £100 to ransom him.'[1]

It was a bad beginning for the King's troops. Northampton immediately called another council, and the watchmen at the gates were commanded to keep their guard more diligently than previously. Sir Edward Ward was made Knight-Marshal and Sir Thomas Paston, Sir John Clare, Sir William Walgrave, Sir Thomas Cornwallis and Sir Henry Bedingfield, all men of 'approved valour and wisdom', were placed in command of different parts of the city. They went about their work, encouraging the men with their words, their presence and sometimes with their own labour. The main body of soldiers encamped in the market-place.

> Gathering great heaps of wood together they set them on fire, lest if anything should happen   on the sudden, they being hindered by the darkness of the night and ignorance of the place, might be encompassed unawares by the enemy.[2]

A few hours later they were all in the midst of battle. Kett had decided quickly that Northampton and his soldiers must be driven out of Norwich. It was intolerable to him that hired ruffians from Italy should be brought into Norfolk to establish law and order over the English peasantry striving for freedom. As for William Parr, Marquis of Northampton, he was neither soldier nor statesman. What respect was due to this courtly parasite, this creature of royalty, who had risen to high place through his sister's marriage with Henry VIII, and his own servility to that monarch? Northampton's knights were landowners, enemies of the people, the very persons against whose authority and tyranny Kett's men had risen.

So, in the dead of night, when the Marquis and his knights were in their sweet sleep in Steward's house, a great attack was made on the city, and for three hours and more the fighting was fierce on both sides. The rebels began with a loud cry and the firing of cannon, and at this the watchmen on the walls and at the gates called, 'To arms! To arms!' Again the cannon did no great harm to anybody, either because they were overcharged in the loading or because of the gunners' lack of skill.[3]

At the first alarm Sir Edward Ward, the Knight-Marshal, roused Lord Northampton, his lords, knights and others, and they all came, in half armour, to the market-place where they remained until daybreak. Alderman Steward was sent to find old Lord Wentworth, Sir Anthony Denny, Sir Ralph Sadler and Sir Richard a Lee, and bring them to take counsel. Sir Richard a Lee, sat in a stall of the market and advised the ramping up of various parts of the walls, especially on the west side of the city. It was obvious to him that with their comparatively small force every man would be needed for active service.

All of a sudden the rebels poured down from Mousehold upon the city, like a rushing stream. They hacked and fired at the gates, they climbed the walls, they swam the river, they pushed in wherever a gap in the old walls was visible. But Northampton's troops held their ground bravely, and Sir Thomas Paston and Sir William Walgrave fought conspicuously to keep the rebels out of Norwich. Kett's men were badly armed but they vastly outnumbered the royal army, and they were fighting desperately for their lives. Defeat meant death at the hangman's hands.

Again and again the rebels came rushing on, crowding the river and swarming around the city walls. No quarter was given on either side and, even when mortally wounded, Kett's men still fought on and struck at their adversaries. Wood's account reads:

> Half dead, drowned in their own and other men's blood, even to the last gasp, they furiously withstood our men. Yea, many also stricken through the breasts with swords and the sinews of their legs cut asunder (I tremble to rehearse it), yet creeping on their knees, were moved with such fury, as they wounded our soldiers, lying amongst the slain almost without life.
>
> For when the force of the enemy abated, the soldiers rushed upon them with such violence that they could no longer abide the fight, or stand to resist; but being overthrown, and beaten down on every side, they were driven out of the city and returned to their camp.[4]

Three hundred of the rebels lost their lives that night, and the city remained untaken. With the enemy repulsed, labourers were set to work to repair the gates, and the Marquis and his staff went to have breakfast at the Maydeshead.[5] For the moment the attack had been beaten off, but Northampton was aware that with so small an army at his disposal the position was extremely precarious. Not only were Kett's forces close at hand and Norwich ill-prepared for a siege, but within the city itself there were so many supporters of the rebellion that, if they should rise, it would be practically impossible to escape disaster. To add to the difficulties, only the wealthy and more important of the townsmen could be relied upon – the burgesses generally waited anxiously for the outcome of the battle before taking sides against Kett. These people had already suffered enough loss through the rising and, while they earnestly yearned for the return of civic peace and quiet and trade, they were not prepared to endanger their lives.

If the Government could put down the rising it would be well and good, but if not it were better to leave Kett in authority than have the city laid waste by the fire and sword of civil war. At present it was not clear whether Northampton or Kett was the stronger, and it occurred to the burgesses that perhaps a promise of pardon might yet induce the bulk of the rebels to disperse. Northampton welcomed the proposal, and so in the morning the herald and a trumpeter were sent down to Pockthorpe Gate, where it was said some 400 or 500 men were to be found.

No man was more delighted than the deputy mayor at the prospect of peace. He joyfully accompanied the herald and the trumpeter to Pockthorpe Gate on the morning of 1st August, only to find to his disappointment no one waiting, neither man, woman, nor child. However, a blast from the trumpet quickly brought a crowd from the hill, led by John Flotman of Beccles, said to be an 'outrageous and busy fellow, a man of voluble tongue ready by nature with reproaches and arrogant speeches'. When Flotman asked what the trumpet call meant, the herald answered:

Go thy way and declare unto thy company from the Marquis of Northampton, governor of the King's forces, that the King's Majesty doth command and admonish them, that now, at length, they repent and put an end to the outrages they were committing: if they will do this, they shall be safe and shall by his clemency be free from peril, and no man shall be charged with the crimes he may have been guilty of.

As Kett was not present, Flotman took it upon himself to make a stout reply to the herald's offer, much along the lines of Kett's own earlier replies to such offers:

I care not a pin's point for my lord Marquis of Northampton, who is a man neither of courage, counsel, nor good fortune. I despise him and hate him as an infamous and worthless man – one always standing in need of others' help – a man guilty of all disloyalty and treason.

As for us, we, for our part, have always been earnest defenders of the King's safety and dignity, and we will ever be ready to spend for his sake all our goods and fortunes.

We have taken up arms not against the King, but for things which we hope will turn out hereafter as much for his welfare as our own. Our consciences do not convict us either of wickedness conceived in our hearts or of treason against the King.

For what is it we desire to do? Is it not to defend the King's name and dignity; to provide for the common safety; to defend the rights of law and liberty; to preserve ourselves, our wives, children, and goods; and finally, to deliver the commonwealth, vexed as it is in so many ways unjustly, from the detestable pride, lust and cruelty of its enemies? Wherefore, being void of offence, we ought naturally to be free from punishment.

A gorgeous herald, emblazoned with gold, has just made us certain offers, and in appearance these are excellent and magnificent. But this has only been done in order that, either by making peace now – a false and treacherous peace at the best – he may restrain your endeavours to recover your liberty, or else, having deprived us of the means wherewith we are now furnished, and so shut us out from all defence, he may deliver us up to a cruel death.

Let those, therefore, who have offended, enjoy the impunity promised; we will not hinder them from so doing. While we are defended by our weapons and by our own innocence we feel ourselves perfectly secure, and will never crave mercy of any man. The commonwealth is now almost utterly overthrown and it is daily declining through the indolence of the 'gentlemen'. Our intention is to restore it to its former dignity out of the miserable ruin in which it hath so long been lying; and either we shall accomplish this by our present course of action, or else, as becomes brave and high-spirited men, we will fight boldly, risk our lives, and, if it be so, perish on the battlefield. Liberty may suffer much at the hands of oppressors, but never shall her sacred cause be betrayed by us.[6]

Flotman had hardly finished before a fearful outcry arose in the city and the shout was heard, 'To arms! To arms!' While the herald, the deputy mayor and Flotman were making speeches at Pockthorpe Gate, the rebels had again attacked the city, and this time they forced an entry by the hospital meadows. The herald's business thus came to an abrupt end and he fled over Whitefriars Bridge.

Deputy Mayor Steward rode another way into Tombland to see what was happening, and in the plain before the gate of the bishop's palace the Lord Lieutenant's soldiers fought with the rebels.

The fight was fiercest between Bishopsgate and the Cathedral, and by noon the King's troops had come off worse. Lord Sheffield fell in the battle, slain by a stalwart rebel named Fulke, a butcher and carpenter by trade, who was hanged after the rising had been suppressed. Bedingfield and Cornwallis were taken prisoners by Kett.

Sheffield's death was the turning point in the fight. It heartened the rebels, and as the army from Mousehold kept pouring into the city in an apparently endless stream, the soldiers became demoralised and at last fled in hopeless confusion. On hearing of

Sheffield's death, Northampton's troops began to languish. Wood's account is characteristically partisan:

> Insomuch that when the rebels, puffed up with exceeding joy, making a mighty alarm on every side, as having already gotten the victory, rushed into the city (by what way they could get in), following upon our men and as mortal enemies setting upon them, they being partly overcharged with the multitude (for they were almost 20,000 and ours were only 1,500), and partly stricken with the death of this noble young gentleman, went out of the city, and (escaping by divers journeys through byways, hiding themselves all the night in caves, groves and woods) returned at the length all of them to London.

By noon the battle was over and Northampton was in full flight. The total loss of life was not great. Sotherton estimated it 'above 40 persons' and added that 'many of the Lord Lieutenant's men departed sore hurt'. According to King Edward's Journal, the Marquis departed with the loss of 100 men, and Nevylle declares that the number was '140 of the enemy slain, and some of our soldiers.'

The city suffered badly in this conflict, but it could hardly have been otherwise. Houses were set ablaze in Holme Street (now Bishopbridge Street) and the city gates were burnt in the hour of victory. Many of the wealthier citizens fled hastily from Norwich, leaving their families and their goods to the mercy of the rebels while, according to Sotherton, others 'hid their gold, silver plate and household stuff whatsoever they possessed, in wells, ponds and other secret places, that it might not be helping to the rebels thereafter'.[7]

Deputy Mayor Steward remained in the city, shutting himself up alone in his big house and brooding in despair on what was taking place. This was until a party of Kett's men came knocking at the door to know if Lord Northampton was hiding in the house. Alderman Steward was in great trouble on that 1st August. He had welcomed Lord Northampton and disavowed the rebels, and now the rebels were in command of the city and the deputy mayor was of no more account than its mayor. Steward entered his house while Northampton and his troops were fleeing in disorder:

> Doubtful what to do, and finding his servants departed with the army, seeing the city empty of all assistance and every man's door shut, comfortless, with a heavy heart went up alone to his highest gallery.[8]

Looking out over the city, Steward saw that the rebels had set all the houses in Holme Street on fire, along with a large part of the Hospital, Bishop's gates and the gates and houses of Pockthorpe, Magdalene, St Austins', Conisford, and Bearstreet.[9] Nevylle, in piteous language, describes the day of Kett's triumph over the King's troops:

> Lamentable and miserable was the state of the city: when nothing was seen or heard, but lamentation and weeping of those that were vexed and troubled: and on the other side the rejoicing of the enemy; the weeping of women, the crying of men and the noise of those that ran about the streets; then the clashing of weapons, the flames of the burning, the ruin and fall of houses, and many other fearful things which (that I may not tell in full) I willingly let pass, which so filled with horror, not only the minds and eyes of the beholders, but struck with incredible sorrow the hearts and ears of all that heard it.[10]

The fire spread with fearful rapidity as most of the dwelling-houses were thatched, but fortunately for the citizens it was extinguished by a heavy fall of rain.

The prosperous burgesses were bitterly dismayed at Kett's triumph. They could not bring themselves to work with the rebel leader and were without the will to make any resistance. Those who were able left Norwich, while the rest stayed at home and moaned feebly of their plight. It is small wonder that some of the shops of the rich tradesmen were looted in the days that followed the victory. Civic authority had crumbled to dust, Kett had a thousand responsibilities on hand, and it was a day or two before the rebels woke up to the necessity of re-establishing order and preserving the city from attack.

It was impossible to re-appoint Steward as deputy mayor, but Kett chose some of his own men for aldermen and constables, and arranged for watch to be kept every day at the gates, the prisons, and other important places. Some of the citizens who remained were brought in for this duty. Steward was obliged to help in enrolling citizens to act as watchmen, and he endeavoured to the last to keep up the religious services at the Oak. He procured Dr Barrett and other preachers to go up among the rebels and preach God's word. However, this did not help as no one could restrain them. The time had long gone when preachers of patience and moderate counsel would be listened to as they deserved.

For three weeks Robert Kett had the rule of Norwich, and beyond loss of trade and the inevitable open robbery of the rich men in the city, who for the most part had run away, there was both respect for life and fairly good order all that time. The good burgesses, of course, were in a state of great anxiety, and the city seemed pitiful in the extreme. So hard and hopeless seemed their lot that some of the burgesses were even moved to repentance and a 'holy life'.

It was not enough that the citizens were compelled to take their turn as sentries; they and their servants were obliged to minister to the wants of Mousehold Camp.

The women resorted twice a day to prayer, and the servants (except what must needs stay at home) did the same. When Kett's ambassadors were sent to any private house they were fain to bake or brew or do any work for the camp, else they were carried as traitors to the Oak. As for trading, there was none in the city, people being forced to hide up their choicest goods, and happy were they that had the faithfulest servants.

They that did open their shops were robbed and spoiled, and their goods were measured by the arm's length and dispersed among the rebels; their children they sent away for fear of fire. I, the writer (who was then above twenty-two years of age and an eyewitness) was present after prayer during this dolorous state, when people met and bewailed the miserable state they were in, and like to be in, holding up their hands to heaven, praying with tears that God would deal so mercifully with them, that they might live to talk of it, thinking it impossible at that time, they were so devoid of hope.[11]

The general feeling of the trading classes in the city was of utter hopelessness, and all who had property were dispirited under Kett's rule.

There was no hope that any citizen looked for to enjoy his own; such as had trusty servants caused their goods, bonds, stuff and money to be made up in walls and cellars, for that they looked with fire to be consumed: the masters themselves in many places were seen to be concealed in false roofs and other secret places, lest if they had been taken prisoners, as other gentlemen were, they should be driven to join the rebels.[12]

To join the rebels, and assist in helping the landless peasantry to end the enclosures, was the last thing on the mind of the respectable citizens. All they wanted was to be allowed to trade and grow rich in peace and quiet.

The servants of the fugitive burgesses were faithful to their masters. Kett declared that all who had fled the city were to be held as traitors and open enemies of the King's Majesty, and their goods to be confiscated, yet many of the servants baked bread and pasties, and roasted meat for the rebels to save the rest of their masters' goods. This plan seems to have been successful – 'the hungry people being pacified, were somewhat stayed from their plundering'.[13]

In all their misery, and in spite of their heavy losses, the Norwich traders were in no danger of their lives. Kett would not allow anyone to be killed except in battle. The mayor and aldermen had thwarted his plans, the wealthy citizens had done their worst to hinder and discourage the rising, but Robert Kett did not consider revenge. He spared the lives of both the landowners and the citizens, but because he needed to take toll of their goods he reaped only hatred for his pains.

VII

THE RISING FAILS IN THE COUNTY

'Robert Kett was not a mere craftsman: he was a man of substance, the owner of several manors: his conduct throughout was marked by considerable generosity: nor can the name of patriot be denied to him who deserted the class to which he might have belonged or aspired, and cast in his lot with the suffering people.' – Canon Dixon, *History of the Church of England*

CHAPTER VII:

The Rising Fails in the County

In those three weeks of August, Kett waited anxiously at Mousehold for the rising to become widespread, but he was disappointed by the lack of success of the lieutenants he had despatched.

In July the country people rose round Lynn, Downham and Swaffham and made a camp near Castle Rising. Driven from there by the landowners, who were not so timid as those in Wymondham and Norwich, the peasants moved south and made another camp at Watton. Here they stayed for a fortnight, holding the river at Brandon Ferry and Thetford. They seem to have been without leaders, and so in early August Watton was abandoned and the rebels there came to join Kett's army on Mousehold.

At Cambridge the people had also risen, simultaneously with the Norfolk men, and on 10th July they pulled down the fences erected at Barnwell by one Bailiff Smyth. However, the mayor, the vice-chancellor and certain heads of colleges went out to confront the rebels who were finally pacified. On 13th July, Somerset wrote a long letter to the vice-chancellor and mayor, in approval of what had been done, and urging the redress of recent unlawful enclosures.[1]

On 16th July, Somerset sent a promise of pardon to Cecil for the Cambridge rebels:

> We have received your letters of the fifteenth of this instant, and thereby understand your request for a pardon to be granted to certain persons lately offending within the county of Cambridge, whereunto upon hope of their amendment we are conformable. And to that end we send you herewith their pardon, upon the proclaiming whereof we will ye declare the King's Majesty's bountiful mercy and goodness

towards them, being moved with pity upon this their first offence; and upon the committing of the like not to trust for his Majesty's mercy to be showed unto them, but for his princely power and sword to be extended against them as a scourge to rebels. And perceiving amendment upon this admonition, his Majesty will accept and use them as any other his faithful subjects not committing the like offences.[2]

The promises of pardon and of the redress of grievances ended the trouble at Cambridge. However, there is an item in the town treasurer's accounts from this time, 'for carrying out of gallows and a new rope', which suggests that 'his Majesty's mercy' was not too widely extended after the pacification. Towards the end of July a rebel camp was also set up near Hingham, although this was attacked boldly, if unsuccessfully by Sir Edmund Knyvett and his retainers who only just managed to escape.

The rebels then went to Kett to report their losses. Having consulted with him it was proposed that they should attack Sir Edmund at Buckenham Castle, in order to force him out. However, there was considerable dissension among the leaders as the place was well fortified and some thought it was too strong to be taken. Others were held back by their fears as the castle was twelve miles from the main camp. So that enterprise was dropped.

At Hingham, as at Castle Rising, Watton and Cambridge, the weakness amongst the peasants was the absence of responsible leaders. Kett alone displayed any real powers of generalship, and he could rely on a number of good fighting men in his camp and on many faithful lieutenants.

The hardest disappointment to Kett came from Yarmouth. On the first news of the camp at Mousehold some of the Suffolk people, notably of Beccles and Bungay, had risen and marched swiftly to Yarmouth. There they captured John Millicent and Nicholas Fenn, the town bailiffs; but these two soon escaped, and as the townsfolk refused to admit the rebels or to sympathise with the revolt, the Suffolk men withdrew to Mousehold.

Sir Thomas Wodehouse reported to the King's Council that Yarmouth was loyal to the Crown, and on 26th July Somerset wrote congratulating the bailiffs and urging them to be on the alert. A week after the despatch of Somerset's letter, by which time Northampton had been defeated, Kett made a strong attempt to win over Yarmouth. He sent a commissioner with one hundred men and authority to take command at the port.

As on previous occasions the official letter was signed by old Alderman Aldrich, who was still on good terms with Kett, and whose name, they might have thought, would carry weight with the constitutionally-minded. (Cod was no longer signing and, in fact, was heard of no more while the rising lasted.)

Nicholas Byron our commissioner in this behalf. Be it known to all men, that we Robert Kett and Thomas Aldrich, commissioners of the King's Camp at Mousehold, have appointed out of our camp aforesaid, one hundred of men to return from us to Yarmouth, for the maintenance of the King's town there against our enemies.

Also we do certify you, that we, for the more sufficient and necessary victualling of our said 100 men, do appoint Richard Smith, Thomas Clarke and John Rotherham, and also to take up horses for the further aiding of our said men.

Dated at the King's Great Camp at Mousehold the 5th day of August in the 3rd year of the reign of our Sovereign Lord King Edward the Sixth.

By me Robert Kett
By me Thomas Aldrich

But Yarmouth showed no respect either to this commission or to its bearer. The townsfolk declined altogether to admit any of Kett's men or to grant supplies to Mousehold, and instead sent off three burgesses to London where they were received in royal audience. On 6th August Somerset wrote that he would:

Very shortly and by main force weed and try out our good subjects from the evil, to minister aid and comfort to the one, and contrariwise to extend the rigour and extremity of our sword to the other.

He exhorted them to continue the guard of the town until he arrived, for at that time the Protector himself was proposing to take command of the next expedition into Norfolk.

Kett continued to send proclamations to Yarmouth, ordering various matters as though the town acknowledged his authority. But Yarmouth was stubborn. It ignored Kett's commands and threats, and was unmoved even though Northampton had been routed.

Kett then decided to take the town by storm. This attack took place on 17th August. A large body of rebels reached the island of Lovingland, and with cannon from Lowestoft came right up to the very walls of Yarmouth, only to be repulsed. Russell reports their failure:

This being perceived, a party of townsmen were privately detached to set fire to a large stack of hay on the west side of the haven, which being duly executed, raised a prodigious smoke, and the wind being northerly, drove the said smoke directly upon the face of the enemy, which so blinded them, that they did not perceive the Yarmouth men coming upon them; whereby many of the rebels being unprepared, were slain and thirty taken prisoners, who, with the six pieces of ordnance, were immediately brought to Yarmouth, and confined in close hold.

The rest, being exceedingly irritated by the above disaster, dared to approach the very walls of the town and to destroy as much as possible all the materials for the new haven, then in making across the Denes near the south gate, to which they did irreparable damages; but being driven thence by the ordnance from the walls and mounts, they fled and never appeared about the town afterwards.[3]

And that was the end of all Kett's hopes of rousing Yarmouth to insurrection. The town took considerable pains to exclude and defeat the rebels and to notify the Lords of the Council in London of its loyalty. Years later, in an address to Queen Elizabeth's Privy Council, the Yarmouth Corporation recalled its resolution and the injuries the town had suffered:

> The said Kett with his rebels made attempt to take that town for their hold, which the inhabitants of that town would in no wise permit, or consent unto, but kept the town for the King's Majesty according to their allegiance, albeit Kett and the rebels besieged it, summoning and threatening it with fire and sword; nevertheless the said townsmen not only kept them out but drove them away, and took certain great ordnance from them, which they had gotten from Lowestoft and other places; and also they did slay, kill and wound many of the said rebels: the which things the said rebels did revenge upon the said town of Yarmouth by spoiling the works of their haven and stopping it up in the night times.[4]

Repulsed at Yarmouth, Kett could now look for help nowhere other than from his own army at Mousehold. No communications came to him from other parts of the country; no promise of any early remedy for the ills of the countryside reached him from the throne. Yarmouth had appealed to London against the rebel leader, the Norwich citizens had implored help against him, and on every side the local risings had been dispersed.

It was a grim prospect facing Robert Kett in those hot mid-August days. On the 10th of August, by royal proclamation, Somerset was declared to be in command of the army that was to put down the revolt. The King's proclamation, announcing Somerset's command, called on various persons to be ready in a week's time to march against the rebels.

One copy ran as follows:

Whereas one Kett, a tanner, supported by great number of vile and idle persons, hath taken upon him our royal power and dignity, and calleth himself master and king of Norfolk and Suffolk, with derogation of our Imperial Crown and Majesty, and not content to persuade our subjects, whom we were well contented to receive to our mercy, to refuse our most gracious pardon, but causeth also a great number of our honest and good subjects to follow and aid him, and so continueth the rebellion in most vile sort, killing, spoiling and keeping in fetters and chains gentlemen, serving-men, yeomen and farmers, and other honest men, who have regard for their faith and duty unto us, robbing ladies' and widows' houses, seeking nothing but spoil and subversion of us and the good estate of the realm. We have appointed our most entirely beloved uncle the Duke of Somerset, governor of our person and protector of our realms, dominions, and subjects, with an army royal to go against them, and with God's help to subdue them to the terror of all others, whom like us we have appointed to march forward with all speed possible. So having reposed a special trust and confidence in your good towardness and readiness to serve us, we have appointed you to give your attendance upon our said Uncle, and therefore do will and require you immediately, upon the sight hereof, with all speed to put yourself in a readiness with an hundred able men, or so many more as ye are able to make and may trust unto you of your servants, tenants and friends, well furnished with armour and weapon, whereof so many to be demi-lances or light horsemen, as ye can furnish, with able and good horses and other convenient furniture, to be at our town of Waldon in our county of Essex the 17th day of this present month at the furthest: at which time and place order shall be given for the bringing of them thither to your contentation, requiring you not to fail as ye tender our pleasure and will answer for the contrary at your perils.

Given under our signet at our palace of Westminster the 10th day of August the third year of our reign.

P. Somerset[5]

But Somerset found it impossible to take the command as this would have alienated the popular support which his domestic policy had brought him. A week later another proclamation called upon the gentlemen of East Anglia to leave London and prepare to wait upon the Earl of Warwick.

We know from Warwick's letter to Cecil, dated 11th August, in which he strongly requested that Northampton should retain his commission, that the command was already in Warwick's hands.[6]

Five days later the expedition had started, and on 21st August the Earl of Warwick was at Cambridge.

VIII

THE EARL OF WARWICK AT NORWICH

'That a populous and wealthy city like Norwich should have been for three weeks in the hands of 20,000 rebels and should have escaped utter pillage and ruin, speaks highly for the rebel leaders.' – *Victoria County History of Norfolk*

CHAPTER VIII:

The Earl of Warwick at Norwich

The Earl of Warwick was a man of vastly different calibre from his friend the Marquis of Northampton. The latter was no soldier, whereas John Dudley, Earl of Warwick, was resolute, ambitious and experienced in warfare. He was created Earl of Warwick and Lord Great Chamberlain on the death of Henry VIII, and had distinguished himself in the expedition against the Scots in 1547. He was now on the eve of accomplishing Somerset's fall from power and ruling the Council as his successor. Unscrupulous and pitiless, with none of Somerset's sympathy for the common people, Warwick was to enjoy the brief triumph of his ambition, to order the execution of his rival, and then in his turn perish on the scaffold.[1]

Warwick was plainly the man to put down the Norfolk rising. Although Kett had made no movement southward, the disaster of Northampton and the power of Kett's 'commonwealth' at Norwich threatened the authority of the Royal Council. Somerset could do no more to check or redress the wrongs of the people as he was already in danger of losing office and his life. The Protector had ordered the discontented peasantry to return to their homes under a promise of pardon, but they had refused to obey. Since rebellion persisted, the sword must do its work for the safety of the realm.

There was to be no repetition of Northampton's failure, and Warwick set out from London with a great number of lords, knights, squires and gentlemen, carrying a substantial store of armour, munition, shot and powder. He had with him native and foreign troops, whose number was said to be 12,000. Lord Northampton, Warwick's two sons, Ambrose Dudley and Robert Dudley (afterwards Earl of Leicester – the favourite of Queen

Elizabeth), Sir Thomas Gresham, and Sir Edmund Knyvet, were amongst Warwick's officers. The mercenaries were German.

The army moved with great speed and reached Cambridge by 20th August. Here Warwick was met by a deputation of fugitive aldermen and citizens from Norwich, who fell to their knees weeping and began a piteous tale of woe. According to Wood, they begged the Earl not to punish them, as they were guilty of no crime and had suffered at the hands of the rebels. In the end, to save their lives, they were forced to flee the city, and with sword and fire were cast out. The reply to this rather sorry exhibition was a mild rebuke and pardon, with advice to follow the army.[2]

Leaving Cambridge the march was resumed and on 22nd August the army, strengthened by reinforcements of country squires, was at Wymondham. On the following day they were at Intwood, some three miles south of Norwich. Here Warwick rested at Sir Thomas Gresham's fine large house, old Intwood Hall, and on the morning of 24th August sent a herald to announce that war would be made against the city unless the gates were opened to the King's army.

The news of Warwick's approach, and that a captain with armour, soldiers and all the instruments of war, had been sent against them, struck no fear into the hearts of Kett's men. It only stirred them to arm, train and fortify themselves to make resistance. Kett, hearing that a herald was at St Stephen's Gate, directed Augustine Steward, the deputy mayor, and Alderman Robert Rugg to learn the herald's business. So the two aldermen met the herald and were informed that the Earl of Warwick, the King's lieutenant, was waiting to be received by the city. On hearing this the aldermen could only bemoan their own unhappy lot and implore the Earl to repeat the promise of pardon for those who would disperse.

The herald at once carried the aldermen's appeal to Warwick who, impressed by the idea that so dangerous and dreadful a flame might be quenched without slaughter and bloodshed, determined to try an offer of pardon. All Warwick cared about was the break up of the rebellion. If this could be done without battle so much the better, for the rebels were strong enough to make the outcome no certain victory for the King's troops. There was also the fear that in the event of open hostilities – whatever the result – the rebels might decide to kill all their prisoners.

So after a quarter of an hour the herald was back at St Stephen's Gate, accompanied by a trumpeter. The portcullis was raised, the gates thrown open and the herald, the trumpeter and the two aldermen, with thirty or forty of Kett's men on horseback, went in procession to Bishop's Bridge Gate – the gate closest to the camp. Here they halted and, after the trumpet had sounded, great numbers of rebels came flocking down from the hill to form a crowd so huge that it covered an area of a quarter of a mile. The people were all in great good humour and cheered lustily: 'God save King Edward! God save King Edward!' When the aldermen had got the crowd quiet, the herald, in full dress, delivered his message at considerable length.[3]

First he harangued those who had wickedly taken up arms against their country. How long, he demanded, 'would they continue to adorn with counterfeit titles the foul impiety of mischievous treason and wrap in the false garments of seeming virtue their horrible foulness and villainy?' He cautioned them to consider their enterprise of destruction, slaughter, wasting, burning and stealing. He threatened them that the 'sea of evils' into which they had thrown themselves headlong had offended and displeased the King and that he had determined to remove the 'foul evil abiding in the bowels of his kingdom' and not to leave them unpunished and unrevenged. He appointed the Earl of Warwick to pursue the conspirators with fire and sword. However, such was his great bounty and clemency that for one last time he would offer mercy to those who desisted in their wickedness. Those who would not would receive the fully merited punishment of God and the King.[4]

This speech was received with extreme disfavour by the rebels. A few trembled in fear, but most of those who heard what was said broke out in angry shouts and curses. Some denied that he was a real King's herald at all, and called him a traitor sent from the landowners to lull them with flattering words and fair promises in order to deceive them. Others declared that the pardon only appeared good and liberal but would prove fatal, for in reality it was nothing more than 'barrels filled with ropes and halters.'[5] The herald's gorgeous coat was resented, and cries went up that it was made of old church vestments, and that the gentry had given him a piece of an old cope for his coat armour. Threats were uttered against him, 'while all round about poured forth the bitterness of their venom in cruel speeches, savouring of death itself.'[6]

Then Robert Kett himself came on the scene and the disorder ended, for Kett took the herald away to a spot near the river so that he might proclaim his message to those who, because of the number of people, had been unable to hear him before.

It was during the second speech of the herald that trouble began. A boy made an indecent gesture at the herald, and a soldier who had crossed the river was so incensed by this that he shot at the boy with an arrow. The boy fell dead. Immediately the cry of 'treachery' was raised by the people, and a dozen or so horsemen went galloping to Mousehold, saying: 'Our men are killed by the waterside.'[7] The herald turned to Kett. It was useless to go on exhorting this excitable mob and the only chance was to get Robert Kett to make peace in the name of his followers. Would Kett come with him under a flag of truce to the Earl of Warwick?

The herald moved off quickly and Kett went with him as far as the bottom of Stuart Hill. In those few minutes the rebel leader hesitated. He knew that Warwick was at hand with a formidable army and that his own men were ill-armed. There was no hope now that the rising would spread; nowhere except at Mousehold and in Norwich had the revolt been successful. Further resistance meant much bloodshed and loss of life, and could he hope to win any redress for the peasants unless help was forthcoming? And yet he was not included in the general pardon, and what assurance was there that peace would bring security to his followers, or that the promise of pardon would be fulfilled? Too often, in the past, the promises of a king and his ministers had been broken. Too often the laying down of arms had been followed by ruthless executions.

While Kett stood in anxious doubt a number of his men came tearing up, calling out, 'Whither away, whither away, Mr Kett? If you go we will go with you, and with you will live and die.' Others beseached their captain not to forsake them.

Kett thereupon made his irrevocable decision. He and his men would fight it out to the bitter end. As the herald began to get alarmed at the increasing numbers of those gathering, and at their demeanour, he implored Kett to go back and calm his men. Kett at once complied.

So the herald set off to report the failure of his mission to the Earl of Warwick, and Kett retired to Mousehold to prepare for battle.

Warwick was satisfied that neither by entreaty nor fair promises, nor even by fear of punishment, could the rebels be turned from their enterprise, so he brought his troops quickly to the city. The portcullis was closed at St Stephen's Gate, but a master gunner fired and broke the half-gate and portcullis. Lord Northampton and Captain Drury, who had previously distinguished himself in the Government service when commanding a body of soldiers in Suffolk, entered, scoured the streets, and killed various rebels.

Warwick, with his main army, entered at St Benet's and came straight to the market-place. Here he began re-establishing the King's authority by promptly hanging sixty men whom he found in the city, without hearing their cause. They were rebels, and that was cause enough.

At three o'clock on the afternoon of Saturday 24th August the artillery went astray. While Warwick was busy in the market-place hanging rebels and delighting the hearts of loyal citizens, the great bulk of his guns and ammunition arrived at St Benet's Gate and followed the army into the city. But the drivers of the gun-carriages did not know the road, and instead of turning right when they reached Charing Cross, to enter the market-place, they went straight on to Tombland. They crossed St Martin's Palace Plain, and actually passed out of the city at Bishop's Gate on the very road to Mousehold. Here they were easy prey to Kett's men who, with great rejoicing (as they had been completely without these things) carried into their camp the carts laden with guns and powder. The formidable Captain Drury, hearing of the mishap, went promptly in pursuit, and a skirmish occurred at Bishop's Gate, with no great result.

Kett had now a distinct advantage in artillery and his men were in good spirits. Warwick had his army in the market-place, but the rebels were also in the city in great numbers. The main body was in Tombland and ready to take the offensive, for they believed that the King's troops could be routed just as Northampton's had been. In the late afternoon the rebels in the city divided themselves into three companies, and began to assemble in the many lanes where they thought they might cut off their enemies. One company was near St Michael's, Coslany; another by St Simon's Church, Elm Hill, and St Peter's, Hungate, by the Elm and on the Hill at the corner; a third was at St Andrew's Hall (previously the Black Friars). All were in battle dress, and there was serious fighting in the streets before nightfall. In addition to these three companies the rebels had friends in every part of the city.

The rebels began by cutting off a handful of soldiers who had strayed from the marketplace, and three or four 'gentlemen' were slain before help arrived. Warwick promptly moved off to take vengeance, leaving only a few Welshmen to guard what cannon he had. At St Andrew's, Warwick's troops were greeted with a heavy discharge of arrows from Kett's bowmen; Wood described it as 'a mighty force of arrows like flakes of snow in a tempest'. However, the arrival of Captain Drury, fresh from Bishop's Gate, turned the tide. The captain had a company of gunners, 'young men of excellent courage and skill,' as Wood depicted them, 'who payed them home again with such a terrible volley of shot, as if it had been a storm of hail, and put them all to flight.'[8]

More than 300 were killed on both sides in this engagement, in addition to the men whom the soldiers found creeping in neighbouring churchyards and under the walls, and put to death. The main body of the rebels retreated from the city, and the fight was over within half an hour.

Against this defeat Kett could place a successful sally against the Welsh gunners. Some of the rebels had noticed the small size of the guard left in charge of the artillery and, in Warwick's absence from St Andrew's, they rushed in considerable force on the astonished and terrified Welshmen. A man named Miles, very skilful in discharging ordnance, led the charge and shot the King's master gunner. The rest, some unarmed, others armed with staves, bills and pitchforks, ran down the hill and made an assault upon the Welshmen. At the first encounter they left the baggage and carts and ran away on all sides with a great deal of noise and speed.

This blow, following the capture of the misdirected artillery earlier in the afternoon, was very harmful to Warwick's men. The arms were needed, and Kett's gunners discharged the ordnance they had taken and battered the city grievously. Most of the guns were set up outside Bishop's Gate and Conisford Gate. By the evening of 24th August, Warwick was within the city and Kett had withdrawn to Mousehold, but it was hard to say who was likely to be the victor.

All the next day, Sunday 25th August, there was fighting in the streets in the south part of the city and houses were set aflame, while a fierce cannonade raged at Bishop's Gate. Warwick was determined to hold Bishop's Gate against invasion, and appointed Lord Willoughby to guard that street and gate. The previous night he had taken what steps were possible to watch and fortify any place where the enemy might enter the city, but his forces had not been strong enough to prevent an incursion at Conisford, near the gate.

Warwick was at Steward's house in Tombland when, at about ten o'clock on the Sunday morning, news was brought that the rebels were making an entry at Conisford, and that some of them had crossed the river and were burning the houses on both sides of

Conisford Street (now called King Street). They had also burned corn merchandise and stuff stored at the Common Staith. Their advance was checked, but the fires were left unextinguished as Warwick was afraid of withdrawing his men from the middle of the city.

Then came another unexpected attack by Kett's men, from the north. They pushed on as far as the bridges, but were driven back by the soldiers. This caused Warwick to order the complete destruction of White Friar's Bridge and the other bridges to the north of the city.[9]

The citizens now seemed in a worse situation than ever. They saw their bridges broken, their gates destroyed and their houses in flames, and they remembered the fate of Northampton's army. It was too evident to the burgesses, knowing from past experience the power of Kett's army, that Warwick's forces were not strong enough to save the city and that it would be better for the Earl to depart before things became worse. It was better to be governed by Kett than to have the whole city detroyed.[10] Filled with despair and fear, the citizens came to Warwick and humbly begged him to leave the city for his own safety, as his men were outnumbered and the enemy powerful and angry.

But Warwick knew that reinforcements were on the road and would not consider defeat:

Being a man of great and invincible courage, valiant and mighty in arms, and one that thought scorn of the least infamy, he replied: 'What are ye so soon dismayed? And is so great a mist on the sudden come over your minds, which hath taken away the edge of your courage, that you would either desire this thing, or think it can come to pass while I am alive, that I should forsake the city? I will first suffer fire, sword, finally all extremity, before I will bring such a stain of infamy and shame, either upon myself or you.' [11]

To clinch matters Warwick drew his sword, along with the rest of the nobles gathered there, and, reported Wood:

> Commanded after a warlike manner that they should kiss one another's sword, making the sign of the holy cross, and by an oath and solemn promise by word of mouth, every man to bind himself to the other, not to depart from the city before they had utterly banished the enemy, or else fighting manfully had bestowed their lives cheerfully for the King's Majesty.

And so, having thus set his seal on resistance, and trusting in the arrival of more troops, Warwick went on to arrange for the billeting of his men. He had his arms put up at his headquarters at Steward's house, and 'the ragged staff' remained on the gates and doors of the house in token of the Earl's victory. For the rest of that Sunday the enemy were kept at bay.

On Monday, the 26th August, came the welcome news that the expected reinforcements, 1,400 German 'lanznechts', were nearby.

IX

THE END OF THE RISING

'The next day being the 26th of August, 1400 Switzers, good and valiant soldiers, came from London and entered Norwich, and were received by the Earl's forces with many vollies of shot and joy.' – Blomefield, *History of Norfolk*

'So ended the Norfolk rebellion, remarkable among other things for the order which was observed among the people during the seven weeks of lawlessness.' – J. A. Froude, *History of England*

CHAPTER IX:

The End of the Rising

The Earl of Warwick was at dinner when the relief arrived, and the spirits of both troops and citizens were revived by the presence of more than 1,000 trained soldiers. Shots were fired in joy, and hospitality was freely offered to the German mercenaries who had come to put down the rebellious English peasantry. There was no longer any talk of asking Warwick to depart, and confidence was expressed that now at last Kett and his rebels would be overpowered.

The city aldermen and burgesses entertained the lanzknechts and their wives, and Warwick's tired soldiers fired volleys in gladness of heart. Meanwhile, Robert Kett and his men at Mousehold condemned themselves to destruction, because it was on that Monday that the fatal decision was made to leave the high wooded ground where the camp was placed, and to come down and do battle in a valley north of the city.

On Mousehold Heath the rebels had the advantage, and a victorious resistance might have been made had Warwick's army attacked. On open, level ground the advantage was on the side of the professional soldier. The only excuse for going down into the meadows and taking the offensive was the need for securing a free passage through the city for provisions for the camp. In Kett's mind there may also have been anxiety to defeat Warwick before further reinforcements arrived.

Certain old rhymes were freely quoted by the peasants, and were viewed as prophecies of victory. Two, in particular, were repeated throughout the camp and accepted as proof of success. One ran:

> The country gnoffes, Hob, Dick, and Hick,
> With clubs and clouted shoon
> Shall fill the vale

Of Dussindale
With slaughter'd bodies soon.

Sadly for the countrymen on Mousehold, the vale was to be filled with their own slaughtered bodies, not with those of their enemies.

Another verse received equal respect as an utterance of prophecy:

The heedless men within the dale
Shall there be slain both great and small.

And slain these heedless men were who left their strong defence on Mousehold – lured to their death on the strength of these vain predictions. One omen spoke against the departure from the camp. Wood reported that a snake 'leaping out of a rotten tree, did spring directly into the bosom of Kett's wife'. This reportedly struck many men with fear and deeply concerned Kett.[1]

With cheerful belief that victory was before them, and in the highest spirits, the rebels broke their camp at Mousehold:

All their dens and lurking-places everywhere, which they had made on Mousehold of timber and other provision, were now set on fire, and the smoke rising from so many places, distant one from another, seemed to bring night almost upon the whole skies and covered the plains with thick darkness. This was to be no mere sally against the royal troops, to-morrow they would utterly destroy their enemies, and the city of Norwich and the whole county should henceforth be their camp.[2]

On Monday night the march began, and twenty banners and ensigns of war were carried to Dussin's dale, the spot predicted for victory by the prophets.

It is impossible to place Dussin's dale exactly, but we know from the Indictment that the battle was fought in the parishes of Sprowston or Thorpe. The open, low-lying ground to the north-east of the city, beyond the walls, about a mile from Mousehold, may be taken as the most probable scene of Kett's disaster. Sotherton reports the movements of Kett's men on the Tuesday morning of the 27th August:

> The rebels had removed their ordinance and munition and all other things clean from that place they were in before, and devised trenches and stakes wherein they and theirs were intrenched, and set up great bulwarks of defence before and about, and placed their ordinance all about them. That the gentlemen – the prisoners – should not escape, they took them out of their prisons in Surrey place and carried them to Dussin's dale with them, which was not past a mile off.[3]

To strengthen their position the rebels also dug a ditch across the highway, and cut off all passage.

Warwick, learning of the departure from Mousehold, promptly set out to do battle. Taking 1,000 Germans and all his horsemen, and leaving the English foot soldiers in the town, he crossed Coslany Bridge and left the city by the gate of St Martin's at the Oak. He was accompanied by the Marquis of Northampton, Lord Willoughby, Lord Grey of Powis, Lord Bray (who had fought in France for Henry VIII) and Ambrose Dudley.

Outside the city, Warwick made another appeal to the rebels to surrender, promising pardon to all except the ringleaders and threatening vengeance if they persisted in war. Sir Edmund Knyvet, Sir Thomas Palmer and two others were sent on ahead to offer the now customary terms. But to all this the people answered stoutly that they would not give up their purpose.

Warwick, on the failure of this mission, turned to his troops and told them to treat the rebels not as men, but as brute beasts to be exterminated:

Invade the enemy valiantly, and without doubting, take and regard the company of rebels before you, not for men, but for brute beasts, indued with all cruelty. Do not let them suppose that they are coming out to fight, but to take punishment, and at your hands these most ungratious robbers speedily require it. They are the bane of their country, set on overthrowing Christian religion and duty – to be laid even with the ground, afflicted, punished and utterly rooted out. In short, these rebels are the most cruel beasts, and they strive with incurable madness against the King's Majesty.[4]

The soldiers were eager for battle and accepted their commander's view of the rebels, so the fight was soon raging.

At the first charge of Warwick's cavalry, Kett's lines were broken in confusion. The rebels had placed their prisoners, chained together, in the forefront, but not one of them is known to have been slain. Miles, Kett's master gunner, a daring and courageous man who had been conspicuous in the city at the capture of Warwick's guns, killed the royal standard-bearer with an iron bullet early in the battle. Warwick's horsemen then charged with terrific force, and at the same time the mercenaries fired with a volley of shots that made Kett's front ranks turn and flee, enabling the prisoners to escape to Warwick's lines.

The nerve of Robert Kett failed him on that critical day and he was powerless. He had sanctioned the departure from Mousehold against his better judgment, and his will seems to have been paralysed by the sense of impending doom. He was exhausted with the strain of the long responsibility. It was plain from that first charge that his men could not stand against Warwick's professional soldiers, and the crude trenches, hastily thrown up in the valley, could not stop the onward rush of these trained and disciplined troops. Again and again an attempt was made to rally the beaten men, but the onslaught was too great. Until now the rebels had been on the attack, but in Dussin's dale they were driven like sheep and pounded to death. On the level ground,

Kett's army could not face the assault and, as Wood reports, the battle speedily became a massacre:

Instead of abiding the encounter, they like sheep confusedly ran away headlong as quickly as they could. But through the noise and cry of our men following, even now in the last obstinacy of treason...they with deadly obstinacy withstood our men a little while: such, however, was the force of the shot and the eagerness of our men to rush upon them (for like unbridled horses, being greedy of the victory, they broke into the host of the enemy), that Kett's army being beaten down with the hot assault and overthrown on every side, were almost with no labour driven from their standing.[5]

Early in the afternoon, when all was lost, Robert Kett rode quietly away from the field. The rising was over, and for him there could be no pardon. The only hope of safety lay in flight.

With the courage of despair and in the midst of disorderly retreat, a last stand was made by one body of rebels. Someone called out, 'Better die manfully in fight, than be killed like sheep as we run,' and at these words a recovery took place. A barricade was hastily erected, and a considerable number of men stood ready to maintain their ground. 'They swore, each to the other, to lay down their lives manfully in that place or else, in the end, to get the victory'.[6]

Warwick, perhaps in recognition of the courage of these men, sent a herald to promise pardon to all who surrendered, and to announce that no mercy would be shown to those who continued to fight. The rebels, with the recent hangings in the market-place in their minds, had confidence neither in the herald, nor in Warwick's mercy, and replied firmly that they would rather die fighting than yield:

They would willingly lay down their weapons, they said, if they were persuaded that that promise of impunity would prove their safety; but they had had already experience of his cruelty upon their companions, which was to them an undoubted sign, as they firmly believed, that the mention of pardon, deceitfully offered by the nobles, was made only in order that they should all at the last be led to torture and death. And, that in truth, whatsoever might be pretended, they knew well and perceived this pardon to be nothing else but a cask full of ropes and halters, and therefore die they would.[7]

Warwick was reluctant to prolong the battle and sent word that he would come and give his promise in person, if they would then lay down their arms. They all answered that if he did this, they would believe him and resign themselves to the will and authority of the King.

It seemed to the remnant of the rebel army that, if this was a real promise of pardon, there was nothing left for them but to surrender. Their leader was gone. Thousands of their comrades were dead or dying around them, thousands were being hunted to death as fugitives. It was better to die in honest fight than to be butchered like sheep, but it might be better to live than to die in battle.[8]

So Warwick came out to the barricade and ordered the herald to read the King's commission, with its promise of pardon to all who submitted. Trusting the pardon, which was most solemnly promised to all, they laid down their weapons. With one voice they thankfully cried, 'God save King Edward! God save King Edward!'

This was the end of the battle. It was then four o'clock and, with the surrender of this last body of men, Warwick's victory was complete. It was not just defeat of the rebels, it was a thorough annihilation of their army. With their own hands the rebels had destroyed their secure camp on Mousehold; they had offered themselves for slaughter by going down into the meadows and now, in the late afternoon of 27th August, they were beaten by the King's troops. The rising was crushed, the good fight put up for liberty by the peasants was finished. Kett's army was broken to pieces by the move from Mousehold to the meadows, and the hope of the country folk died with the insurrection.

There was great rejoicing in the city that evening at Warwick's victory. Two barrels of beer were provided by the Corporation at the cost of twelve shillings, and, according to the City Chamberlain's Accounts, the liquor was 'drank at the market cross amongst the soldiers as they came home out of the field after it was won.' All the booty of the rebels was also given to the soldiers, and they promptly sold it in the city market.

That same evening Robert Kett was taken. Riding from the battlefield he had gone north, hoping, perhaps, to reach the coast. But at Swannington, only eight miles from Norwich, both horse and rider were too tired to go farther, and here Kett took refuge in a barn. He was so tired that only when he had laid down to rest did he notice a cart full of hay nearby, with men unloading it. Before he could move, the rebel leader was recognised and the men seized him. Weary and heavy of heart, Kett made no resistance. They brought him to the house of Master Richards while they fetched Mrs Richards from church. Kett made no attempt at flight. Mrs Richards, on her arrival, berated him for his conduct, but he only prayed her to be quiet and to give him some meat.

The summer night descended on Robert Kett, worn to breaking point, a captive in the house of Mr Richards, and on the dead and dying in Dussin's dale, and the peasants, fugitive and dispirited, and in prison. It also descended on victorious Warwick and his mercenaries, and on Norwich burgesses, exulting that the rebellion had at last been put down, well away from the city.

Very early next morning Robert Kett was taken as a prisoner to the Earl of Warwick's lodging.[9]

X

AFTER THE RISING

'So ended the Norfolk rising like every other peasants' revolt, in disillusion and defeat. The stars in their courses fought against them; it was not possible to restore an agricultural system which was economically wasteful and effete, and it is always hard to restrain the greed of those who control the govemment.' – Pollard, *Political History*

CHAPTER X:

After the Rising

Warwick returned to the city in triumph after the battle. And now the citizens who, on Sunday, had begged the Earl to depart, on the Tuesday evening praised him enthusiastically.

The clamour for the blood of the defeated peasants began immediately the result of the battle at Dussin's dale was known, and the value of the royal promises of pardon was quickly seen.

On the morning of the 28th August the executions began, and throughout that day the hangman was kept busy. Nine of the bravest of the peasants, including Miles who had slain the King's standard-bearer, were taken to the Oak of Reformation where they were hanged, disembowelled alive, beheaded and quartered. 'These are the judgments of traitors in our country,' said Sotherton. The severed heads were fixed on the tops of the towers of the city and the rest of the body scattered in several places to terrify others.

Then 300 peasants were hanged on trees outside the city and left for the birds to feed on. In Norwich itself 49 prisoners were hanged in the market-place. It meant nothing to the Earl of Warwick that these prisoners had surrendered on the often repeated promise of the King's pardon.

All that day the cry was sent up for more executions:

Many of the gentlemen, carried away with displeasure and desire of revenge, laboured to stir up the mind of Warwick to cruelty. Not contented with the punishment of a few they would have rooted out utterly the offspring... [1]

Even the Earl of Warwick, hard and unscrupulous as he was, shrank with disgust from the vindictive savagery that called out for a general massacre of the prisoners. Besides, if all the peasants were killed, who would do the agricultural work in the country? He turned on the squires and burgesses impatiently:

> There must be measure kept, and above all things, in punishment with death men must beware lest they exceed. I know well such wicked doings deserve no small revenge, and that the offenders are worthy to be most sharply chastised. But yet, how far shall we go? Are we never to be satisfied? Is there no place of pardon? Shall we hold the plough ourselves, and harrow over our own lands? [2]

For weeks Robert Kett and his army held the lives of land-owners and aldermen in their hands, and showed mercy. But no voice was raised to remember the humaneness of the rebels. Neither justice nor pity was given to the peasants.

The common-sense of Warwick's speech had effect. The bodies of the executed were buried beyond Magdalen Gate that same night, in case they might produce infection or sickness.

The appetite for blood had been satisfied (if rather too moderately for some) and Warwick declared the executions at an end. On the following day, the 29th August, the Earl with all his nobles, knights and squires, and a great company of men and women of all ranks and ages, went to the church of St Peter's, Mancroft. Here they offered their prayers and praises to Almighty God for their success.

It was decreed that this service should become an annual matter. It was further decreed that in every parish, with the service over, a solemn peal of all the bells should be given, and a sermon preached. The ordinances of mayors and councils are not meant to endure for ever, but this service of thanksgiving 'for the deliverance of the city from Kett's rebellion' was performed as late as 1667.

Warwick remained in Norwich until 7th September, then departed for London taking with him Robert and William Kett as captives.

The landowners continued to make accusations against certain rebels, not so much now for the purpose of seeing them hanged, but in order to obtain a share in the confiscated properties, as the Ketts were not the only men of moderate substance who had taken up arms at Mousehold.

Sir Thomas Wodehouse, writing from Wroxham to his brother in London on 3rd September, refers to these proceedings:

> You shall understand that my lord of Warwick doth execution of many men at Norwich. And the gentlemen crave at his hand the gift of the riches of them, and do daily bring in men by accusation. But I have neither accused any man, nor yet have asked the gift of any, although I am spoiled of 2000 sheep and all my bullocks and horses with the most part of all my corn in the country. All the ordnance and spoil that was taken in the camp is the King's. I moved my lord for my two pieces of brass, but I cannot have them at his hands, yet he is very gentle to me.[3]

The citizens continued to praise Warwick for the preservation of their lives and those of their wives and children, and all their goods and possessions. They did this ignoring the fact that their wives and children, and the great bulk of their goods and possessions, had been quite unhurt during the weeks of Kett's supremacy in Norwich. The city fathers also spent seven shillings for setting up the Warwick's arms (the 'ragged staff') in silver leaf beside the King's arms at all the gates of the city.

At length Warwick, with high affairs of State before him, was free to leave. The rebellion was over. The landowners could return to their estates, Steward, Cod, and their fellow-aldermen could resume the peaceful government of the city, and the peasants wandered homeless as before.

Robert Kett and his brother were secure in the Tower of London by the 9th September.[4] Their trial opened on the 23rd November, and on the 26th November they were found guilty of high treason and condemned to a traitor's death.

In that October 1549, while the Ketts were prisoners, William, whose part in the rising had been comparatively small, was allowed to walk freely in the Tower. Meanwhile Warwick, fresh from his Norfolk triumph, overthrew Protector Somerset and became the chief power in the realm. On the 12th October Warwick arranged for Somerset to be arrested by order of the Council, and on the 14th the Protector was brought to the Tower, to remain the fellow-prisoner of Robert Kett.

The formal charge against Robert Kett declared that he had made an insurrection and levied war against the King. On the 20th of July, and for the ensuing six weeks, he gathered 20,000 men on Mousehold Heath, and caused bills to be written inciting people to levy open war against the King. In this charge he was accused of robbing the King's faithful subjects, imprisoning knights, esquires, and gentlemen at Mount Surrey and, on the 27th of August, killing many faithful subjects of the King at Dussin's dale.

The charge against William Kett was in very similar words. He had 'excited rebellion, and insurrection', and on the 16th of August, and two following days, had conspired with Robert Kett 'to destroy the people'. Also, on the 20th day of August he 'gave Robert Kett and the other traitors comfort, aid, and counsel in their traitorous designs'.[5]

Both men pleaded guilty to the indictments against them, and no defence was offered. What defence was possible? Kett had taken up arms without royal permission, he had endeavoured to do the work of King and Parliament in his county of Norfolk, and he had resisted, successfully for a time at least, the forces of the Crown. His work had come to nothing; his own mistake on that fatal Monday when the camp was broken up had brought the movement to its end. But still there was the memory of those few good weeks when he had done justice at the Oak; when the mighty had been tumbled from their seats and the poor and the disinherited had lived in freedom, and the earth and its fulness had been restored to the common people.

To plead 'not guilty' was to deny these things. If to strive forcibly for the rights of the landless was to be a traitor to the King, then Robert Kett was unmistakably a traitor. Fate had conspired against him, and to escape a traitor's death was impossible. As he had faced life courageously and dared to voyage on dangerous waters, so would Robert Kett face death calmly. To die a traitor was to pay the penalty of defeat. A few years more and both Protector Somerset and the Earl of Warwick himself would die as traitors.

On the 26th of November the capital sentence, with all its horrors, was pronounced against Robert and William Kett. They were not taken to Tyburn as the sentence decreed, but three days later were delivered out of the custody of the Tower to the keeping of Sir Edmund Windham, High Sheriff of Norfolk, to be taken by him to execution in their native county. Then came a hurried journey back to Norfolk, and on 1st December the Sheriff and his prisoners were in Norwich.

It was hot summer-time when Kett had ruled at Mousehold and when he had fled from Dussin's dale. And now, on his return, it was bleak winter and all the countryside looked dreary, cold and lifeless.

For six days Robert Kett was left in shackles in the Guildhall, and then on the morning of the 7th December he was drawn through the streets on a rough hurdle to Norwich Castle. There he was hanged in chains over the walls of the castle, according to the King's command. On the same day William Kett was hanged in chains from the top of Wymondham Church tower.

And so the Ketts, having fought the fight, and having kept the faith they had pledged to the peasant folk of Norfolk, passed from the hands of sheriffs and hangmen to the rest that remains   for both victor and vanquished. True, their bodies were denied the quiet of the grave, and swung uneasily for many days – preaching, to all who passed by, the end that awaits the loser in social and political revolt. Failure was the witness of these gibbeted figures on Norwich Castle and Wymondham Church.

The mournful creaking of the chains, the despised and rotting bodies atoning for the deeds of the strong mind and resolute will they had once housed, the constant, visible presence of death in the very midst of the people; these all proclaimed the failure of rebellion. Who could pass by Norwich Castle, or gather to prayer in the old church at Wymondham, and not see the broken flesh fluttering in the wind? The children would learn that the ghastly scarecrow swinging in the air was all that was left of the mighty Kett, the man who had so recently held sway over Norwich and all around, and who had dared to meddle with Government and set himself above the landowners of the country.

Yet there were some who could not look at the poor body, high above the castle, without seeing it as a pennant of the good cause, a torn banner of the fight for freedom. They would gaze on it with reverence as upon the tattered flag of a famous regiment hanging, when its work is done, in the quiet of a great church. Country people coming to market were moved to pity and were heard to say strange things:

> John Redhead, of St Martin's Parish, worsted weaver, saith, that upon a market day, not a month passed, he saw two or three persons, men of the country standing together, and he heard the one of them speak to the other, looking upon Norwich Castle towards Kett, these words: 'Oh! Kett, God have mercy upon thy soul, and I trust in God, that the King's Majesty and his council shall be informed on it betwixt this and midsummer even, that of their gentleness thou shalt be taken down, by the grace of God, and buried, and not hanged up for winter store; and set a quietness in the realm; and the ragged staff shall be taken down also of their own gentleness from the gentlemen's gates in this city, and to have no more King's arms but one within this city under Christ, but King Edward VI, God save his grace.'[6]

But the civic authorities were not idle. Kett would become no popular hero if they could help it. If the infamy of his death and the spectacle of his rotting flesh were not sufficient, then abuse must be heaped upon his name and reputation.

To ensure this, an account of the rising, written in Latin by one Nevylle, was published in 1575 and ordered to be used as a text-book in the Grammar School, replacing the works of classical authors. This version of the story, called *De Furoribus Norfolciensum*, was used for several years. Based mainly on Sotherton's manuscript, and violently anti-popular in tone, it is full of the fiercest epithets against Kett and his men.

The bodies were left hanging until (in Robert Kett's case at least) they had literally fallen to pieces in corruption. On 13th January the inquest was held in the Guildhall in Norwich. Here it was shown that the property of Robert Kett consisted of the Manor of Wymondham, obtained by grant from the Earl of Warwick in 1546, and valued at £4 per annum; certain lands formerly belonging to the Hospital of Burton Lazars, also obtained from Warwick, and valued with two tenements, at Cakewick Field near the marlepits at Wymondham, at 20 shillings per annum; and the manors of Melior's Hall and Lether's Hall, called Gunvill's Manor, valued at £13. 6s. 8d. per annum, and mortgaged to Richard Colyer for £200.

All this property was confiscated under the death sentence, and on 18th May 1550 it was granted by the crown to Thomas Audley, 'in consideration of the good, true, faithful and magnanimous services lately performed for us in the contest with our unnatural subjects in Norfolk.'[7] Audley is not mentioned as having taken part in any battle against the rebels, but he was responsible for taking Kett on the journey from Norwich to London.

So the last echoes of the rebellion passed, and Thomas Audley came into possession of the lands Kett vacated when he started out from Wymondham on that bold march to Mousehold.

The rising failed, and was doomed to failure quite apart from the disastrous move to Dussin's dale. It was too exclusively an agrarian revolt. Kett looked for support in the towns, without success. Weavers and cobblers might sympathise with the peasants, but the prosperous citizens of Norwich did not care about the enclosures that drove thousands off the land. On the contrary, shrewd burgesses saw that there was more profit to be made from sheep and wool than from the cultivation of the soil, and more profit meant more trade, more business, more money. It did not matter to them that people were dispossessed, and driven from the fields their fathers had tilled, to become vagabonds in the countryside, if sheep or cattle could bring money to the nearest towns. Mayor Cod and Alderman Steward, and the townsmen of Yarmouth and other places, were content that Kett and his rebellious peasants should die, if trade advanced. It was only the poorer workmen who suffered from the rise in the price of foodstuffs.

The movement also lacked the wide organisation of the years preceding the Great Uprising in 1381. At this time John Ball and preaching friars had carried a common message of revolt from village to village, binding the peasants together in clubs and unions to prepare for a day of restitution. Similarly, in those early years of Edward VI the rural people seethed in discontent, the whole countryside in anger against the enclosures, or against the changes in religion. However, there was neither unity nor method in the various insurrections. The risings were all local, and the lack of communication between the counties was fatal to national success.

There was also a lack of leadership in most places. Robert Kett did everything that one man could do in Norfolk and, proving himself in a thousand ways, was trusted completely by the people. But in no other county was a leader such as Kett to be found, and the smaller risings in Norfolk and elsewhere collapsed because they were ill led. All rebels in Norfolk and Suffolk came to Mousehold as they had no confidence in anyone but Kett. We do not even know the names of the peasant leaders elsewhere in 1549; in 1381 it was quite the opposite. Kett must have counted on the co-operation of other popular leaders, as Wat Tyler did, but he was disappointed.

The Norfolk Rising was the last great revolutionary movement of the common people in England. The Civil War was mainly an affair of the middle class and the nobility, while ignoring the social question. Riots and mob violence may occasionally exist even in our own day, but never since 1549 have the people risen to redress their wrongs by force of arms.

After the Norfolk Rising the town and country labourer sank lower and lower. The enclosures went on unhindered, and in the latter part of the eighteenth, and early nineteenth century, when the commons that had survived earlier extinction were absorbed by the landowners, no rising took place, and no strong protest was made. All feeling for liberty was dead in the labouring people, and although they could still prove their endurance and bravery as soldiers and sailors, a brutish ignorance hung over the land.

Only in the nineteenth century did the social question once again agitate the people, and resolution was made to end the oppression and miseries of the poor. However, the working-class leaders in England realised that this could only be achieved by parliamentary legislation, not fighting. The weapons have changed, but the old cry for social justice uttered by Robert Kett still rings in our ears; that the possession of English land by the few, to the exclusion of the many, must end.

* * * * *

The Duke of Somerset survived Robert Kett by two years, and went to the scaffold in January 1552. Eighteen months later, John Dudley, Earl of Warwick and now Duke of Northumberland, proclaimed his daughter-in-law, Lady Jane Grey, Queen of England. He called on East Anglia to support her claim, but there was no response; neither peasant nor landowner would follow him. Norfolk rallied to the standard of Queen Mary, and the executioner of Somerset was, in his turn, brought to the scaffold.

On 22nd August 1553 – just four years after his victorious entry into Norwich – Warwick died, as his father before him had died, a traitor's death by the executioner's axe, on Tower Hill. And never was a traitor's death less honoured in England. The title of Earl of Warwick became extinct in 1581 with the death of his son Ambrose who, although married three times, was childless.

The Kett family has flourished in Norfolk. There are many good citizens bearing that name at the present time in Norwich, and the churchyard at Wymondham shows the burial-place of more than one descendant of the famous rebel.

NOTES

Chapter 1
1. Cheney, Social Changes
2. Pollard, England under Protector Somerset
3. Strype's Memorials
4. Pollard, op. cit.
5. Froude, History of England
6. State papers, Edward VI, Domestic
7. See Appendix - Somerset's Proclamation Against Enclosures
8. Strype's Memorials
9. Many popular ballads of the time express approval of the pulling down of hedges and fences:

    'Cast hedge and ditch in the lake
    Fixed with many a stake
    Though it were never so fast
    Yet asunder it is wrest.

    Sir, I think that this work
    Is as good as to build a kirk,
    For Cambridge bailies truly
    Give ill example to the country:
    Their commons likewise for to engross
    And from poor men it enclose.'

    See C. H. Cooper, Annals of Cambridge
10. State Papers, Edward VI, Domestic

Chapter 2
1. From Blomefield, History of Norfolk. He adds: 'This very thing was, in a measure, the beginning of the rebellion; for the Ketts, who were chiefly concerned in the purchase, and were very desirous of saving the church, being at that time the principal inhabitants, never forgave Flowerdew, but endeavoured to do him and his family all the prejudices imaginable ever after.'
2. Nevylle, De Furoribus Norfolciensum (1575), later translated into English by Wood, 1615.
3. Nevylle, op. cit.
4. Nevylle, op. cit.
5. Nevylle, op. cit.

Chapter 3
1. Nevylle, op.cit.
2. ibid.
3. F. W. Russell, Kett's Rebellion

Chapter 4
1. It is impossible to identify the site of the Oak. The rebels occupied a very wide area of the heath.
2. Aldrich lived at Mangreen Hall, Swardestone, and was Mayor of Norwich in 1507 and 1516. He died in 1559.
3. See Appendix for the Petition in full.
4. Haywood, Life of Edward VI
5. See Appendix for Somerset's reply in full.
6. Haywood, op.cit.
7. Nevylle, op. cit.
8. Wood's translation of Nevylle.
9. Wood
10. According to Russell, Parker was 'respected exceedingly'.
    Clayton comments that this may have been the case in Norwich, but at the Oak it was not exactly conspicuous.

Chapter 5
1. Sotherton, op. cit.
2. ibid
3. Wood
4. 'Our Captain Kett and his soldiers entreat of this city, and of you the Mayor and your brethren, peace and truce for a few days whereby we may have liberty (as the custom was of late) to transport victual through the city, which thing except ye grant, we will break into the city by force and destroy it with fire and sword.' – Nevylle.
5. Clayton comments: 'It is difficult to believe this speech was really delivered by Cod. The city at that time had not been seriously damaged, and its mayor had not been imprisoned. Possibly Cod in after years made out that he gave this valliant reply, and so Nevylle put it down as authentic.'
6. Sotherton, op. cit.
7. Sotherton, op. cit.
8. Clayton comments: 'It is probable that the names would have been known had any of the citizens died at Mousehold.'
9. Steward, a mercer by trade, was three times Mayor of Norwich, 1534, 1546 and 1556, and MP in 1541. Bacon, a grocer, was Mayor in 1556.
10. Nevylle, op.cit.

11.   ibid

Chapter 6
1.   By 'a wretched rebel, one Cayme of Bungay,' according to Sotherton.
2.   Sotherton
3.   Although Russell contends that some thought the gunners had been bribed to fire too high.
4.   Wood
5.   The Maid's Head inn
6.   This is Wood's account. Sotherton is content to say that Flotman 'defied the Lord Lieutenant and said he was a traitor ... but they were the King's true subjects.'
7.   Sotherton, op.cit.
8.   ibid
9.   ibid
10.   Nevylle
11.   The Norwich Roll – quoted by F. W. Russell, op. cit.
12.   Sotherton, op.cit.
13.   ibid

Chapter 7
1.   C. H. Cooper, Annals of Cambridge
2.   ibid
3.   F. W. Russell
4.   Swinden, History of Great Yarmouth
5.   Cotton MSS. Vespasian, F.iii.37
6.   State Papers, Edward VI . Warwich wrote: '...if it might please your grace to use his service again, I shall be glad for my part to join with him; yea, rather than fail, with all my heart to serve under him for this journey, as I would be to have the whole authority myself.'

Chapter 8
1.   'The subtlest intriguer in English history.' – A. F. Pollard, op. cit.
2.   ibid
3.   See Appendix IV for Wood's account of the Herald's pronouncement.
4.   According to Sotherton, Kett was excluded by name from the pardon: 'If they would like natural subjects repent of their demeanour and humbly submit themselves to the King's mercy, his highness would grant unto them pardon for life and goods, Kett only excepted.'
5.   Wood
6.   Sotherton
7.   ibid

8. ibid
9. According to Sotherton the bridges at Fye, Blackfriars, and Coslany would also have been destroyed by Warwick's command, had not the citizens persuaded him otherwise.
10. Wood reports their mood: 'Great astonishment and sorrow struck many men's minds,' so that 'languishing through despair and fear, they almost fainted, now devoid of all counsel.'
11. Wood

Chapter 9

1. Wood. This is the only reference to Kett's wife throughout the rising, nor is there any allusion to the presence of women and children in the camp.
2. Wood
3. Sotherton
4. Nevylle
5. Wood
6. Nevylle
7. Nevylle
8. According to F. W. Russell, 3,500 were slain. Edward VI, in his Journal, puts the number at 2,000. Somerset, writing to Hoby on 1st September, puts it at 'more than 1,000'.
9. According to Sotherton, 20 shillings was paid to 'him who apprehended Kett, the rebel' on 3rd February 1550.

Chapter 10

1. Sotherton
2. Wood
3. State Papers, Edward VI, Domestic
4. £50 was paid to Thomas Audley on 8th September , as 'reward for bringing Kett'. – Privy Council Register, Edward VI
5. This reference to 20th August is not clear. According to Holinshed, 'it was generally thought William Kett would have been certain of pardon (he having done but little in these commotions), if he had not played the part of traitorous hypocrite: for upon his submission at first to the Marquis of Northampton, he was sent back to his brother, to persuade him and the rest to yield: though he promised to do so, yet, upon his coming into the camp, and seeing the great multitude about him, he did not only dissuade him from it, but told him the Marquis had but few soldiers with him, and was not able to resist such a force as his.' If Holinshed's statement is true, the 20th should be the 1st of August.
6. F. W. Russell, from The Book of the Mayoralty
7. Patent Rolls, Edward VI

SOMERSET'S PROCLAMATION
AGAINST ENCLOSURES

1st June 1548

Forasmuch as the King's Majesty, the lord protector's grace, and the rest of his Privy Council have been advertised and put in remembrance as well by divers supplications and pitiful complaints of his Majesty's poor subjects, as also by other wise discreet men, having care to the good order of the Realm, that of late by the enclosing of lands and arable grounds, in divers and sundry places of the Realm, many have been driven to extreme poverty, and compelled to leave the places where they were born, and to seek them livings in other countries, with great misery and poverty insomuch that whereas in time past, ten, twenty and in some places 100 or 200 Christian people hath been inhabiting and kept household, to the bringing forth and nourishing of youth, and to the replenishing and fulfilling of His Majesty's Realm with faithful subjects who might serve both Almighty God, and the King's Majesty to the defence of this realm, now there is nothing kept but sheep or bullocks. All that land which heretofore was tilled and occupied with so many men, and did bring forth not only divers families in work and labour, but also capons, hens, chickens, small pigs and other such furniture of the markets, is now got by insatiable greediness of mind into one or two men's hands, and scarcely dwelt upon by one poor shepherd. So that the Realm thereby is brought to a miraculous desolation: houses decayed, parishes diminished, the force of the Realm weakened, and Christian people by the greedy covetousness of some men eaten up and devoured by brute beasts, and driven from their houses by sheep and bullocks. And that although the same thing many sundry complaints and lamentations hath been heretofore made, and by the most wise and discreet princes his Majesty's father and grandfather, the Kings of the most famous memory, King Henry VII and King Henry VIII, with the consent and assent of the lords spiritual and temporal in divers parliaments, divers and sundry laws and acts of parliament, and most godly ordinances in their several times have been made for the remedy thereof, yet the most insatiable covetousness of men doth not cease daily to encroach hereupon, and more and more to waste the Realm after this sort, bringing arable grounds into pastures, and letting houses, whole families and copyholds to fall down, decay and be waste. Wherefore His Highness is greatly moved both with a pitiful and tender zeal to his most loyal subjects and specially to the poor, which is minded to labour and travail for their livings, and not to live an idle and loitering life; and of a most necessary regard to the surety and defence of his realm, which must be defended against the enemy with force of men, and the multitude of true subjects, not with flocks of sheep and droves of beasts. And further is advertised that by the ungodly and uncharitable means aforesaid, the said sheep and oxen being brought into a few men's hands a great multitude of them being together, and so made great droves and flocks, as well by natural reason, as also it may be justly thought, by the due punishment of God, such uncharitableness: great rots and murrains both of sheep and bullocks hath lately been sent of God, and seen in this Realm, the which should not by all reason so soon fall, if the same were dispersed into divers men's hands, and the said cattle also by all likelihood of truth should be more cheap, being in many men's hands as they be now in few, who may hold them dear, and tarry their advantage in the market. And therefore by advice of his most entirely beloved uncle, the duke of Somerset, governor of his person, and protector of all his Realms, dominions and subjects, and the rest of his Majesty's privy council hath weighed most deeply of all the said things. And upon the aforesaid considerations, and of princely zeal, to see that godly laws made with great travail, and approved by experience, and by the wise heads in the time of the said most prudent princes should not be made in vain but put in use and execution, hath appointed according to the said acts and proclamations a view and enquiry to be made, of all such as contrary to the said acts and godly ordinances, hath made enclosures and pastures of that which was arable ground, or let any house, tenement or meads decay and fall down, or otherwise committed or done anything to the contrary of the good and wholesome articles contained in the said acts, and therefore willeth and commandeth all his loving subjects who knoweth any such defaults and offences contrary to the wealth and profit of this Realm of England, and the said godly laws and acts of parliament done and committed by any person who so ever he or they may be, to insinuate and give information of the offence to the King's Majesty's Commissioners who be appointed to hear the same, so truly and faithfully that neither for fear nor favour they omit to tell the truth of any, nor for displeasure name any man who is not guilty thereof. That a convenient and speedy reformation might be made herein to the honour of God and the King's Majesty, and the wealth and benefit of the whole Realm.

APPENDIX II

THE REQUESTS

We pray your grace that where it is enacted for enclosing, that it be not hurtful to such as have enclosed saffron grounds, for they be greatly chargeable to them, and that from henceforth no man shall enclose any more.[1]

We certify your grace that whereas the lords of the manors hath been charged with certain free rents, the same lords hath sought means to charge the freeholders to pay the same rent, contrary to right.[2]

We pray your grace that no lord of the manor shall common upon the commons.[3]

We pray that priests from henceforth shall purchase no lands, neither free nor bondy: and the lands that they have in possession may be let to temporal men, as they were in the first year of King Henry VII.

We pray that rede ground and meadow ground may be at such price as they were in the first year of King Henry VII.

We pray that all marshes that are holden of the King's majesty by fre rent or of any other, may be again at the price that they were in the first year of King Henry VII.

We pray that all Bushells within your realm be of one stice, that is to say to be in measure VIII gallons.

We pray that priests or vicars that be not able to preach and set forth the word of God to his parishoners may be thereby put from his benefice, and the parishioners there to choose another, or else the patron or lord of the town (to do so).

We pray that the payments of castleward rent, and blanche ferme, and office lands, which hath been accustomed to be gathered of the tenants: whereas we suppose

---

1. The lands where saffron was grown were not to be exempt from the royal proclamation forbidding enclosures.
2. 'Free rent' was the rent due from a lord of the manor to the superior lord from whom he held it: the lord of the manor was bound to pay this himself, and not exact it from his tenants. Curiously enough, William Kett was lord of Chossell's Manor at Wymondham – a small estate belonging to the Earl of Warwick – who obtained it at the Dissolution of the Monasteries.
3. That is, share the common rights of tenants on the common lands.

the lords ought to pay the same to their bailiffs for gathering their rents and not the tenants.[1]

We pray that no man under the degree of a knight or esquire keep a dove house, except it hath been of an old ancient custom.

We pray that all freeholders and copyholders may take the profits of all commons, and the lords not to common nor take profit of the same.

We pray that no Feudatory within your shires shall be a counsellor to any man in his office making, whereby the King shall be truly served, so that a man being of good conscience may be yearly chosen to the same office by the commons of the same shire.[2]

We pray your grace to take all liberty of lete into your own hands, whereby all men may quietly enjoy their commons with all profit.[3]

We pray that copyhold land that is unreasonable rented may go as it did in the first year of King Henry VII; and that at the death of a tenant, or of a sale, the same lands to be charged with an easy fine as a capon or a reasonable [sum] of money for a remembrance.

We pray that no priest shall hold no other office to any man of honour or worship, but only to be resident upon their benefices, whereby their parishioners may be instructed within the laws of God.

We pray that all bond men may be made free, for God made all free with his precious bloodshedding.
We pray that Rivers may be free and common to all men for fishing and passage.

We pray that no man shall be put by your Feudatory to find any office, unless he

---

1. Castleward rents were payments for the upkeep of the king's castles. 'Office lands' were Crown lands. Blanche farms or white rents were the old name for the fixed rents of freeholders of a manor, and were so called because they were paid in silver or white money. Kett objected to the lord of the manor shifting his dues to the Crown on to the tenant.
2. The Feudatory – an officer of the Crown holding a feud or fief – was not to influence elections; and was himself to be appointed by the people and not the Crown.
3. The Court lete of the lord of the manor had extensive powers in the Middle Ages, powers that were later mostly lodged in our Court of Quarter Sessions.

holdeth of your grace in chief, or capite above £10 by year.[1]

We pray that the poor mariners or fishermen may have the whole profits of their fishings – such as porpoises, grampuses, whales, or any great fish – so it be not prejudicial to your grace.

We pray that every proprietary parson or vicar having a benefice of £10 or more by year, shall either by themselves, or by some other person teach poor men's children of their parish the book called the catechism and the primer.

We pray that it be not lawful to the lords of any manor to purchase lands freely[2], and to let them out again by copy or court roll to their great advancement, and to the undoing of your poor subjects.

We pray that no proprietary parson or vicar, in consideration of avoiding trouble and lawsuit between them and their poor parishioners, which they daily do proceed and attempt, shall from henceforth take for the full contents of all the tenthes which now they do receive, but 8d. of the noble (6s. 8d.) in the full discharge of all other tythes.[3]

We pray that no man under the degree of [word missing] shall keep any coines upon any freehold or copyhold unless he pale them in so that it shall not be to the commons' annoyance.

We pray that no person of what estate, degree or condition he be shall from henceforth sell the awardship of any child, but that the same child if he live to his full age shall be at his own choosing concerning his marriage, the King's wards only except.[4]

We pray that no manner of person having a manor of his own, shall be no other lord's bailiff but only his own.[5]

We pray that no lord, knight, or gentleman shall have or take in form any spiritual promotion.

We pray your grace to give license and authority by your gracious commission

---

1. Tenants under £10 were to be excused from holding office for post-mortem examinations and other county business.
2. i.e. that are freehold.
3. A proposal to commute tithes for money payment.
4. A good deal of money was made by the guardianship of children, and by marriage contracts – not to the advantage of the child.
5. A proposal to limit the range of power of landlords.

under your great seal to such commissioners as your poor commons have chosen, or to as many of them as your majesty and your counsell shall appoint and think meet, for to redress and reform all such good laws, statutes, proclamations and all other your proceedings; which hath been hidden by your Justices of your peace, Sheriffs, Feudatories, and other your officers, from your poor commons, since the first year of the reign of your noble grandfather King Henry VII.[1]

We pray that those your officers, which have offended your grace and your commons, and [are] so proved by the complaint of your poor commons, do give unto these poor men so assembled 4d. every day so long as they have remained there.[2]

We pray that no lord, squire, nor gentleman do graze nor feed any bullocks or sheep if he may spend £40 a year by his lands, but only for the provision of his house.

By me,	Robert Kett
By me,	Thomas Cod
By me,	Thomas Aldrich

---

1. This was an appeal to the Crown to sanction the popular representative government set up by Kett – the election of delegates for commissioners from the various Hundreds of Norfolk.
2. A demand for the payment of the people's representatives.

APPENDIX III

THE REPLY OF THE KING BY YORK HERALD
TO KETT'S REQUEST

(Though nominally a royal message, this reply was, of course, the answer of Somerset.)

That, seeing he was always ready to receive and relieve the quiet complaints of any of his subjects, he marvelled much that upon opinion either of necessity in themselves, or of injustice in him, they should first put themselves into arms as a party against him, and then present him with their bold petitions; especially at such a time when, having fully reformed many other matters, he had lately set forth a proclamation against excessive prices of victuals, and had also appointed commissioners with ample authority for reformation of enclosures, of depopulations, of taking away commons, and of divers other things, whereof, doubtless some had been by this time redressed, had not these disorders given impediment to these designs generally; when they might well discern both his care and endeavour to set all matters in a right frame of reformation, as might best stand with his honour and their sureties. Notwithstanding this, however, they were eager violently to take his authority into their own hands.

Touching their particular complaint for reducing farms and lands to their ancient rents, although it could not be done by his ordinary power without a parliament, yet he would so far extend his authority, royal and absolute, as to give charge to his commissioners to travail with all persons within their counties to reduce lands to the same rents whereat they were farmed forty years before, and that rents should be paid at Michaelmas then next ensuing, according to that rate; and that such as would not presently yield to his commissioners for that redress, should, at the parliament which he would forthwith summon be over-ruled.

Concerning their complaint for prices of wools, he would forthwith give order that his commissioners should cause clothiers to take wools, paying only two parts of the price whereat commonly they were sold the year next before; and for the other third part, the owner and the buyer should stand to such order as the Parliament should appoint. At which also he would give order that landed men, to a certain proportion should be neither clothiers nor farmers. And further, that one man should not use divers occupations, nor have plurality of benefices nor of farms; and generally, that then he would give order for all the residue of their requests in such sort as they should have good cause not only to remain quiet, but to pray for him, and to adventure their lives in his service.

This Parliament, he promised, should begin in the beginning of October then next ensuing; against which time they should appoint four or six of their county to present bills of their desires, and in the next season apply themselves to their harvest and other peaceable business at home, and not to drive him to necessity (whereof he would be sorry) by sharper means, to maintain both his own dignity and the common quiet.

FINAL PROCLAMATION BY THE HERALD

They were not ignorant, from the first time ever since they had wickedly taken up arms against their country, how many and sundry waies, by all means possible, labour and study, the King had emploied his care to the end to bring them from the crueltie of these villainies, whereby they had violated all the laws of God and man, to some consideration of their duties and regard of their own safetie; and had sent unto them messengers and proclaimers of peace not once but often, againe and againe. Notwithstanding, they regarded not, but ever despised and by all means misused them through their detestable madness and disloyaltie. But (now, in the sight of God) whither would they rush? Whither would they throw both themselves and their goods with deadly furie? What measure would they put to their most trecherous madnesse? or what ende of their most vile Counsels? How long, being stirred up through pestilent lusts, which they had once suffered to enter their minds, would they, with deadly folly, continue to pursue their false and idle hopes of victory? How long would they adorne with counterfeit titles the foule impietie of mischievous treason? How long would they wrap in the false garments of seeming Virtue their horrible fouleness and villainies? Finally, how long would they be holden bound with the fatal desire of these things, on their obtaining which, if such were allowable, the destruction of the Commonwealth would issue presently much more intolerable and lamentable? But, rather, now at the last instead of acting thus, they should look about them awhile and apply both their minds and understanding, and mark thorouly, with more attentive eyes, their Commonwealth of which in all their talks, no less foolishly than wickedly and ungodly, they were wont to boast. Surely, then may easily be seene whether they be faithful subjects and worthy the name of good citizens; which have taken up hostile arms against the King's Majestie; which have gathered together routs of wicked men despised and vile; which have brought upon their country (the common parent of us all) ungodly and sacrilegious hands; which have let the refuse of the people and the vilest of all mortal men (cast out, for the most part, of all English Society) into the Commonwealth, to the destruction of the good and overthrow of the kingdome; which have defaced with merciless fire the greatest part of this most worthie Citie; which hath laid in most vile prison and bands, many worthy and excellent persons, and have slaine some with most extreme torture; which have utterly emptied the best furnished houses and polled and shaven the neighbouring villages; which have alienated to their own use the goods of many (of late rich men, but now through their crueltie, miserable and needie) and carried them into their wretched Camp by most cruel robberies; which have forged fained laws, false letters and commissions in the King's name; which have profaned the temple of the great and mighty God; overthrown the houses of private men; wasted and spoiled the fields on every side; which have converted all their thought, studies and enterprise to destruction, slaughter, wasting, burning and stealing; finally, which have left nothing remaining, whither the rage and madnesse of their furie could further carrie them, but either their riotous lusts utterly devoured, or their foul importunitie scattered abroad. When they see themselves thus guilty of these so many, so great and so horrible pollutions of wickednesse in the sight of God, their King and the Commonwealth; and when now they see all their goods and substance to be brought into that place, and so confiscate and lost, that to be in a worse condition than now they are in (for they are in the worst) they cannot be, if they would: then, let them think with themselves, into how large a sea of evils they have thrown themselves headlong; and let them think what they may fear, over whose heads alwaies hangeth the just wrath of God (which surely can by no means be avoided) and the inevitable power of the King, offended and displeased. For his Majestie had decreed, not to suffer any longer these so great evils to abide in the bowels of his kingdome, neither to leave any longer unpunished and unrevenged, this so foul cruel tie and intolerable boldnesse. And therefore had chosen the Earle of Warwick (a man of renowned honour and of great name) and unto this work appointed Generall from His Majestie who must pursue them with fire and sword; and hath further injoyned him never to leave off until he had utterly rooted out that vile and horrible company. Notwithstanding, such is his great bounty and clemencie, that whom he hath appointed a revenger of this desperate and wicked rout (if they persevere) the same also he would have to be (if they shall doe otherwise) a messenger and minister of his mercie; the which, except they would embrace it at this time, refusing all sinister advice, Warwick hath most solemnly sworne, shall never hereafter be offered unto any of them againe, but (as he was commanded by the King) he would pursue with fire and sword all the companions of that most pernicious conspiracy, the officers, ministers and abettors thereof, as the most pestilent enemies to the King's Majesty; neither would he make an end of pursuing them, until they (which had defiled all places with their new, unheard of and unpardonable treason, and had drowned themselves in such furious waves of wickedness) had received condigne punishment of God and the King.